CULTURE SMART!
BELGIUM

Mandy Macdonald

Graphic Arts Books

First published in Great Britain 2005
by Kuperard, an imprint of Bravo Ltd.

Series Editor Geoffrey Chesler
Design DW Design

Simultaneously published in the U.S.A. and Canada
by Graphic Arts Center Publishing Company
P. O. Box 10306, Portland, OR 97296-0306

Library of Congress Cataloging-in-Publication Data

Macdonald, Mandy.
  Belgium: a quick guide to culture and etiquette / Mandy Macdonald.
    p. cm. — (Culture smart!)
  Includes bibliographical references and index.
  ISBN 1-55868-904-4 (softbound)
  1. Belgium—Social life and customs. 2. Belgium—Description and
travel. I. Title. II. Series.
  DH677.M35 2005
  949.3—dc22

                              2005009118

Printed in Hong Kong

Cover image: *Light, Air, and Water.* Statue by Bert De Keyser, Zuiderterras,
Antwerp. *Travel Ink/Luc Janssens*

CultureShock!Consulting and **Culture Smart!** guides both contribute
to and regularly feature in the weekly travel program "Fast Track" on
BBC World TV.

About the Author

MANDY MACDONALD is an Australian writer, researcher, and editor living in Scotland. A graduate of Sydney and Cambridge Universities, she specializes in E.U. cooperation with developing countries and gender equality and works for international and European governmental and nongovernmental organizations. She came to love Belgium by living in Brussels in the 1990s and continues to pay regular visits, not only in a professional capacity but also as an amateur musician and performer of Flemish Renaissance music.

Other Books in the Series

- Culture Smart! Argentina
- Culture Smart! Australia
- Culture Smart! Brazil
- Culture Smart! Britain
- Culture Smart! Costa Rica
- Culture Smart! China
- Culture Smart! Czech Republic
- Culture Smart! Denmark
- Culture Smart! Finland
- Culture Smart! France
- Culture Smart! Germany
- Culture Smart! Greece
- Culture Smart! Hong Kong
- Culture Smart! India
- Culture Smart! Ireland
- Culture Smart! Italy
- Culture Smart! Japan
- Culture Smart! Korea
- Culture Smart! Mexico
- Culture Smart! Netherlands
- Culture Smart! Norway
- Culture Smart! Philippines
- Culture Smart! Poland
- Culture Smart! Portugal
- Culture Smart! Russia
- Culture Smart! Singapore
- Culture Smart! Spain
- Culture Smart! Sweden
- Culture Smart! Switzerland
- Culture Smart! Thailand
- Culture Smart! Turkey
- Culture Smart! Ukraine
- Culture Smart! USA
- Culture Smart! Vietnam

Other titles are in preparation. For more information, contact: info@kuperard.co.uk

The publishers would like to thank **CultureShock!Consulting** for its help in researching and developing the concept for this series.

CultureShock!Consulting creates tailor-made seminars and consultancy programs to meet a wide range of corporate, public-sector, and individual needs. Whether delivering courses on multicultural team building in the U.S.A., preparing Chinese engineers for a posting in Europe, training call-center staff in India, or raising the awareness of police forces to the needs of diverse ethnic communities, we provide essential, practical, and powerful skills worldwide to an increasingly international workforce.

For details, visit www.cultureshockconsulting.com

contents

contents

Map of Belgium

introduction

Belgium has somehow acquired the reputation of being Europe's most boring country, a reputation that is entirely undeserved. In fact, if you are looking for the eccentric and the surreal, Belgium is the place to find it.

Perhaps this bland image is a smokescreen, the conventional exterior hiding a subversive sense of humor, a surreal imagination, and a deep-rooted disdain for authority. Or perhaps it is a camouflage, a way in which Belgium, still overrun—however peacefully—by foreigners, can keep a few of its secrets to itself.

The Belgians have been called stolid, pragmatic, self-deprecating, antiauthoritarian, subversive, cautious, and tolerant. Supposedly they eat well, drive badly, have a national inferiority complex, hate paying their taxes, and think rules are there to be ignored. Some of these descriptions are fair, and some are caricatures, as we shall see. Belgians are also generous, kind to strangers, unsnobbish, sarcastically witty, given to practical jokes, and very good at finding solutions to disagreements that will satisfy, or at least mollify, all sides.

It is often said that Belgium has no national identity, only language-based regional or even local identities. After centuries of being fought over, this is hardly surprising. Throughout its history up to independence in 1830 it had been ruled by other European powers, its borders constantly shifting and its fortunes intricately entangled with those of France, Spain, Austria, the Netherlands, and Germany. It is hard not to conclude that the Belgians' disregard for authority figures, rules, and regulations has its roots in centuries of resistance to foreign domination, or that their tendency toward ironic self-deprecation reflects the image of Belgium as being small and unimportant, but nonetheless well worth fighting over. Even the famous "Belgian compromise" can be understood as a response to this constant involvement in other people's conflicts.

Culture Smart! Belgium aims to help you navigate these swirling waters. It is for anyone—businessperson, student, or tourist—who wants to understand Belgian society and encounter it with sensitivity and poise. We trace the land's turbulent history and try to see how the past has shaped the collective and personal values of today's Belgians. We look at the Belgian people at work, at play, and at home, and offer some tips to help you get along with Belgian colleagues and acquaintances without tears—on either side!

Key Facts

Official Names	Koninkrijk België (Dutch), Royaume de Belgique (French)	
Capital City	Brussels	Pop. 1.12 million
Main Cities	Antwerp, Liège, Ghent, Leuven, Bruges, Namur, Charleroi	Common Anglicized forms of place names and regions are used in this book; otherwise, the local form is used.
Area	11,783 sq. miles (30,518 sq. km)	
Climate	Temperate	
Currency	Euro (€)	Belgian franc was replaced in 2002
Population	10.4 million	Population density 333 people/sq. km (1999/2000)
Ethnic Makeup	58% Fleming 31% Walloon 11% other	"Other" includes E.U. nationals, Turkish, Moroccan, and sub-Saharan African immigrants.
National Languages	58% Dutch 32% French 10% German	Dutch is official, but Flemish dialects are also spoken. Walloon and Bruxellois are still used.
Religion	75% Roman Catholic 25% Protestant or other.	"Other" includes Judaism and Islam.
Government	Constitutional monarchy and federal parliamentary democracy with two legislative houses, the Senate and the Chamber of Representatives.	The country is divided into ten provinces (in two regions) and a third region, the capital region, and also into three linguistic communities.

Media	Domestic television includes the Flemish TV1 & Kanaal 2. Main Walloon channels are RTBF1 and ARTE. British, Dutch, and German stations can be picked up. Cable and satellite channels available.	Main newspapers in Flanders: *De Morgen, De Standaard, Het Volk*, and *Het Laatste Nieuws*. In Wallonia: *Le Soir, La Libre Belgique*, and *La Dernière Heure*. The *Grenz Echo* is German-language.
Media: English-language	British and American daily newspapers can be bought from all large railway stations and from some smaller newsdealers.	The weekly *The Bulletin* can be purchased in Brussels. It caters mostly to the expatriate community.
Electricity	220 volts, 50Hz. Standard European two-prong plugs are used.	British appliances need an adaptor; American appliances need an adaptor and a transformer.
Video/TV	Videos use the PAL system.	
Telephone	The country code for Belgium is 32. To dial out of Belgium, dial 00.	There are no area codes in Belgium. All numbers begin with a zero, a throwback to former area codes.
Time Zone	1 hour ahead of GMT; normally 6 hours ahead of U.S. Eastern Standard Time, 9 hours ahead of Pacific Standard Time.	

chapter one

LAND & PEOPLE

"It's quite simple, really, and at the same time rather complicated."

(*Captain Haddock, in Hergé,*
Land of Black Gold)

GEOGRAPHY

Small but perfectly placed, Belgium is the historical meeting point of northern Europe's chief trading routes. It sits on the continent's northwestern seaboard, with several important ports, and borders on the Netherlands, Germany, Luxembourg, and France. Its countryside and cities are diverse, ranging from flat polder land to densely forested mountains and from the slightly museum-like charm of Bruges to the industrial sprawl of Liège.

Covering an area of 11,783 square miles (30,518 sq. km), Belgium has a population of 10.4 million, making it Europe's second-most densely populated country, after the Netherlands. Its landscape naturally divides into three areas: the flat coastal plains of the north, the central rolling hills and river valleys of the Scheldt and the Meuse, and the forested Ardennes Mountains in the south. The highest point, at 2,277 feet (694 m), is the Signal de Botrange, near the town of Eupen.

Running straight for 44 miles (70 km), the coastline consists of long sandy beaches backed by a broad belt of dunes, and beyond them a swathe of low-lying polder land about 10 miles (16 km) across, crisscrossed by many waterways. Although, like the Dutch, the Belgians built a system of drainage dikes and canals, flooding continues to be a threat in these areas of reclaimed coastal land. The Kempen are the lowlands between the rivers Scheldt, Meuse, and Demer, extending east into the Netherlands. These rivers have deposited large amounts of sand and pebbles, creating an infertile landscape clad in pines and heather. The area is largely unpopulated now; in 1952 it became the home of the Center for Nuclear Studies at Mol. Further inland lies the plain of Flanders, traversed by the Scheldt and its tributaries, intensely cultivated and densely  populated. It was here that the textile industry, which is still centered on Ghent and Tournai, developed in the Middle Ages.

In the center, the Haspengouw/Hesbaye Hainaut plateaus are areas of fertile loess covered in heathland, grassland, and coniferous forests. The Brussels Capital Region, at the heart of the country, is a low, fertile loam plateau, gradually rising to 650 feet (200 m) in the south and supporting arable and livestock farming. In the southeast is Belgium's coal-mining area, centered on the towns of Liège and Charleroi.

The Lower Ardennes lie between 650 and 1,650 feet (200–500 m) above sea level and push southward from the Meuse. Further south, the Upper Ardennes is a high plateau sliced through by the wooded valleys of the Meuse and its tributaries. To the east, near the German border, are the peat bogs and moors of the Hautes Fagnes.

In the extreme south is the "Belgian Lorraine," consisting of the Gaume and Arlon regions. Here, along the North Luxembourg escarpment, is the beautiful Anlier Forest of oak and beech. In the Gaume the forests give way to pastures, and with its south-facing aspect and the protection of the Ardennes to the north, the area has a microclimate warmer than the rest of Belgium, giving it the nickname of "Little Provence."

CLIMATE

Belgium's climate is temperate, modified by the North Atlantic Drift and the prevailing westerlies from the sea, with mild, damp winters and cool summers. Inland, however, away from maritime influences, the temperature range is much wider; in the Ardennes, hot summers alternate with cold winters and the area has more rain and snow than elsewhere in the country.

The best time to visit is from May to September. April and November are the wettest months, but in Brussels the rainfall is more uniform. Whenever you visit, it is a good idea to bring rainwear. From November to March the days are often gray and damp, and occasionally snowy, but there is nothing more atmospheric than wandering alongside the frozen, misty canals of Bruges, overhung with willows and lit by a low, pale sun.

A BRIEF HISTORY

Belgium's history has been eventful by any standard—a long story of successive invasions, occupations, fragmentations, and redefinitions. The outline that follows illuminates what makes today's Belgium "Belgian" and distinguishes it from its neighbors, especially the modern Netherlands, with whom it shares so much history.

Prehistory

The earliest inhabitants of Belgium were driven south during the last Ice Age, and people only returned in around 9000 BCE. By the Neolithic period (c. 2600 BCE), agriculture was established, and there is evidence of mining and megalith building. By the Iron Age (around the mid-eighth century BCE), Belgium was inhabited by a Celtic people who by the time of Julius Caesar had formed into several tribes collectively known to the Romans as the Belgae.

Romans and Franks

Caesar called the Belgae "the bravest of all the Gauls," and as the Romans advanced into their territory from 57 BCE, the Belgae resisted them staunchly before being defeated. The region south of the Rhine became the Roman province of Belgica. Here, trading centers grew up alongside new Roman roads, establishing Belgium's role as a mercantile crossroads in northwestern Europe. By the fourth century CE, Christianity was gaining a foothold.

In the fourth and fifth centuries, Germanic Frankish tribes began to push into northern Belgium, unwittingly starting the linguistic divide that splits the country to this day. These northern people retained their Germanic language, in contrast to the Latinized south. When the Roman Empire collapsed, the Franks surged southward, sweeping away both Christianity and the vestiges of Roman civilization.

The Frankish Merovingian dynasty based itself at Tournai. In 496 CE King Clovis embraced Christianity, and the Franks were gradually converted by a series of missionaries. Their kingdom became the center of an empire that reached its peak during the reign of Charlemagne (742–814 CE). The area between the Meuse and the Rhine, centered on his capital at Aachen, formed the hub of a vast Christian realm stretching from the River Elbe to the Ebro in northern Spain.

The Carolingians governed through royal agents, whose descendants came increasingly to identify more with local interests than with those of the king. During the ninth and tenth centuries these local magnates established de facto independence of royal authority. This tendency toward fragmentation was compounded in 843 CE when the empire was divided among the three sons of Louis the Pious. What is now Belgium was given to two of them: Charles the Bald, who received Flanders (a strip of land west of the River Scheldt) as well as most of France, and Lothar, who received the remainder of today's Belgium and lands along the Rhine and the Rhône.

The Counts of Flanders
The partition of Charlemagne's empire opened the way for the ascendancy of a class of nobles who were theoretically subject to the French and

German monarchs but who wielded great power locally. Invasions by both Vikings and Normans in the ninth and tenth centuries consolidated this power. The Frankish rulers put up little defense against the incursions, leaving it to the local lords to protect the populace and in the process step into the power vacuum, becoming feudal masters.

Over the next three centuries the influence of Flanders reached as far as the River Somme in northern France. Baldwin Iron Arm, the first and probably the most powerful count of Flanders, established a stronghold in Ghent in 867 CE, and by the middle of the eleventh century the counts of Flanders were almost independent.

The Growth of Towns and Trade

Monastic communities had begun reclaiming the coastal marshland from the sea, and the medieval landscape from Bruges to the sea and along the Scheldt as far inland as Antwerp was one of polders crisscrossed by protective dikes. From the late eleventh century onward, trade routes developed along the rivers and trading posts gradually became busy, prosperous walled towns. Industry and trade blossomed, particularly in the twelfth and thirteenth centuries. The towns were granted charters by the counts of Flanders. Different regions specialized in different industries: cloth (from wool imported from

England) in Bruges, Ghent, and Ypres, metalworking in the Meuse region of Wallonia. During the thirteenth century merchant ships from across Europe furled their sails in Bruges and Antwerp, and by 1340 Ghent was the second-largest city in Europe, after Paris.

With the emergence of a rich and powerful new merchant class, the cities became independent power bases outside the feudal system. The large population of skilled craftsmen and traders formed powerful guilds and associations and often quarreled with the nobility, whose fundamental allegiance was to the French throne.

By 1322, however, Count Louis of Flanders, a devoted Francophile, had virtually reduced Flanders to a province of France. Edward III of England halted wool exports from England to Flanders, throwing the Flemish cloth industry into crisis. Many skilled workers emigrated—a trend that would recur in later centuries. When the Hundred Years War broke out in 1337, the Flemish sided with their English trading partners rather than their French  political masters, and for much of the rest of the century the guilds and the nobles struggled inconclusively for dominance.

Burgundian Rule and the Flemish Renaissance

In 1398, Flanders joined what is now the Netherlands as part of the Duchy of Burgundy, completing a process that had begun in 1369 with the marriage of Margaret, daughter of Louis of Male, Count of Flanders, to Philip the Bold, Duke of Burgundy. It is at this point, when the bulk of what is now the Netherlands, Belgium, and Luxembourg were brought together under Burgundian rule, that we can perhaps begin talking of the region as "the Low Countries."

Burgundian rule lasted just under a century, but was a time of great prosperity and cultural brilliance. Philip the Good ruled over a territory covering eastern France, modern-day Belgium, the Netherlands, and Luxembourg. His capital was Brussels, though he also held court at Bruges and further afield. In 1464 the regional assemblies of the Low Countries met in Bruges as the "States General" (*Staten Generaal*) to resist Philip's centralizing policies, and as a result of this parliament joint government by the dukes of Burgundy and the States General was established.

Philip's successor, Charles the Bold, continued to unify the regions of Belgium, acquiring Liège in 1468. On Charles's death, his daughter Mary became Duchess of Burgundy. In 1477, she signed the Great Privilege, which restored rights and freedoms to the cities of the Low Countries, making the ruler accountable to them in raising revenue, declaring war, and judicial questions.

Flanders in this period was a hive of intellectual and artistic activity. Ornate Gothic town halls and churches adorned the cities; art and music flourished under the patronage of the Burgundian dukes. Belgium's first university was founded at Leuven in 1425; the great Dutch Humanist scholar Erasmus taught there between 1517 and 1521.

The Habsburgs (1482–1555)

When Mary of Burgundy died in 1482, her widower, the Habsburg Maximilian I of Austria, later Holy Roman Emperor, became regent of the Low Countries. In 1494 he handed the territory to his son, Philip the Handsome, whose marriage to Juana, daughter of the king of Spain, forged a dynastic link between Austria, Spain, and the Low Countries that was to shape Belgium's history for three centuries. Philip's son, Charles V, as Holy Roman Emperor and King of Spain, became the most powerful ruler in Europe, his far-flung possessions embracing not only Spain, the Burgundian Low Countries, and the Austrian Empire, but colonies in Latin America and Asia.

Under Charles's rule, Belgium continued to be a

 center of learning and art and became even more highly urbanized—but trouble was brewing. The Flemish weaving industry was facing competition from England. Within Flanders, the silting up of the Zwin estuary cut off Bruges's trade route to the North Sea, and Charles preferred Antwerp as a commercial and financial center. Worse, he imposed heavy taxes on the towns to finance his military campaigns. In 1540, Ghent (the city of his birth) rebelled, but the revolt was quashed and Ghent's leading citizens humiliated.

Reformation and Revolt (1550–79)

An even darker cloud loomed on the horizon: the upheavals caused by the Reformation and its backlash. Protestantism had gained ground during Charles's reign, especially across the northern Netherlands, challenging the authority and power of the Roman Catholic Church. In 1550, Charles decreed the death penalty for those convicted of heresy; yet Protestantism continued to spread. After Charles retired to a monastery in 1555, his son and successor, Philip II, set out to crush all resistance to Catholicism in the Low Countries.

Philip ruled from Spain and was interested in the Low Countries only for their wealth. He raised taxes yet again. Through his regent, Margaret of Parma, he savagely enforced the anti-Protestant edicts of the Council of Trent. The people, increasingly embracing Calvinism, feared persecution, while the nobility, though mostly Catholics, disagreed with policies that threatened the stability of society and their own prosperity. Together with several other nobles and burghers, both Catholic and Protestant, William of Orange (William the Silent), Burgrave of Antwerp and *stadhouder* for Holland, Utrecht, and Zeeland, resigned from the ruling Council of State and signed the Compromise of Breda, aiming to resist Philip's centralized rule and to rid the Low Countries of the Inquisition. After a bad harvest in 1566, mobs of Anabaptists, Calvinists, and other Protestants rose up and ransacked Catholic churches in "the Iconoclastic Fury." The following year Philip appointed the Duke of Alva governor of the Low Countries and sent him in with 10,000 troops. Under his rule, thousands were slaughtered.

William had gone into exile, where he raised the standard of rebellion. At sea his force of patriotic semi-pirates, known as the "Sea-Beggars," harassed Spanish shipping. Years of religious warfare followed, punctuated by attempts to reach peace and unity, such as the Pacification of Ghent, an agreement signed by Catholics and Protestants on November 8, 1576. The Pacification guaranteed freedom  of belief—a freedom enshrined in the modern Belgian Constitution—in the hopes of ending religious conflict.

In these tumultuous years the boundaries of the modern Netherlands, Belgium, and Luxembourg were drawn. William had sought independence for the entire Low Countries, but the provinces of the south remained loyal to Spain and Catholicism. In 1579 the Protestant north formed the Union of Utrecht, creating the United Provinces of the Netherlands. The southern provinces (roughly modern Belgium and Luxembourg) signed their own pro-Spanish, pro-Catholic accord, the Union of Arras, in the same year.

The Spanish Netherlands (1579–1713)

Brussels was adopted as capital of the Spanish Netherlands in 1585, and the region was ruled by a governor appointed by Philip. Many Protestant traders, craftsmen, and intellectuals fled north, taking their money and knowledge with them. Under Philip's daughter Isabella and her husband, Archduke Albert of Austria, however, the Spanish Netherlands became semiautonomous between

1598 and 1621 and there was a fleeting economic boom, fueled by luxury industries such as lace-making, silk-weaving, and diamond-processing. This was the period of the great painters of Antwerp, Pieter Paul Rubens and Anthony van Dyck, and of the classical philologist and Humanist Justus Lipsius.

This upturn was brief. In 1618 the Thirty Years War, another largely religious conflict between Catholic and Protestant countries, broke out. It ended with the Peace of Westphalia (1648), which included the Treaty of Munster. This forced Philip IV of Spain to concede further territory to the north, including northern Brabant, northern Limburg, and Flemish Zeeland. Under the treaty, the Scheldt estuary was closed to trade, ensuring the decline of Antwerp and the emergence of Amsterdam as the chief port of the region, and both sides granted freedom of belief to each other's citizens. This marks the final split between the northern and southern Low Countries.

With its trade routes strangled, the Spanish Netherlands sank into poverty during the second half of the seventeenth century. Louis XIV of France invaded several times and territory was lost to the northern Netherlands and France. When Charles II of Spain, last of the Spanish Habsburgs, died childless, the remaining territories fell to

France. Two years later, however, the Dutch and
the English disputed France's claim and the War of
the Spanish Succession (1701–13) broke out. In
1713 the territory was handed to the Holy Roman
Emperor, Charles VI of Austria, France retaining
western Flanders, including Lille and Dunkirk.

Austrian Rule (1713–94)

For the rest of the eighteenth century Belgium was
Austrian. When Charles VI died, the European
powers refused to recognize his daughter Maria
Theresa as successor to the Austrian throne. Louis
XV of France briefly occupied the territory before
its return to Austria in 1748.

Maria Theresa's reign saw the economy of the
Austrian Netherlands revive. Roads and waterways
were built, the coal industry was encouraged, and
agriculture was improved. Her son and co-regent
until 1780, Joseph II, was less popular. His
reforms, especially the Edict of Toleration (1781),
were intended to be liberal but in fact upset
everyone from the peasantry to the nobility and
provoked quarrels among conservative Catholic
and pro-republican groups. Eventually, however,
the factions united, drove out the Austrians in
1789 (the "Brabant Revolution"), and formed the
United States of Belgium in 1790. Independence
was short-lived: in 1792 war broke out between
Austria and the newly republican France, and by

1794 Belgium was back under occupation, this time by the French.

The French Occupation (1794–1815)
In this period the foundations of Wallonia's future economy were laid, as it became the most industrialized region in Europe. But the French introduced compulsory military service, persecuted the Church, and abolished the cities' ancient privileges. In Flanders, the Dutch language was outlawed. The Belgians made their by now traditional response, this time in the Peasants' Revolt of 1798, but again were suppressed.

Under Napoleon, from 1799, the reforms continued, although more benevolently. Belgian civil law is still based on the Napoleonic Code. The Church was reconciled, the Dutch blockade of the Scheldt was lifted, and Antwerp came back to life. But the French were hated and it was almost with relief that the populace accepted their next externally imposed regime after Napoleon's defeat at Waterloo in 1815.

Belgium Under Dutch Rule (1815–1830)
At the Congress of Vienna in 1815, the European powers created a buffer state against France by amalgamating Belgium and Holland into the

United Kingdom of the Netherlands. Frederick William of Orange was crowned as its king.

Faced with the task of uniting two countries with different societies and faiths, William I at first did well. He founded schools and universities, promoted industrialization, and gave financial support to entrepreneurs. But he fatally underestimated the strength of entrenched loyalties and rivalries and the extent to which the Flemish had become distinct from the Dutch: he denied southern Belgium fair political representation, alienated the clergy by trying to limit their powers, and (reversing Napoleon's policy) enforced Dutch as the national language, thus enraging both the French-speaking Walloons and the Flemish-speakers in the north, who insisted that their language was *not* Dutch. In fact, the Flemish and Dutch had grown too far apart in religious, cultural, and political terms to reunite.

Revolution broke out rather romantically on August 25, 1830. During the duet "Amour sacré de la patrie" in Auber's opera *La Muette de Portici*, the audience rushed out of Brussels's old Monnaie theater and into the streets, crying "Revolution!" Across Belgium, similar revolts erupted in support of the citizens of Brussels. The Dutch fled, the flag of Brabant was raised over Brussels's town hall, and Belgian independence was recognized at a Conference of Powers in London in June 1831.

Independence

Prince Leopold of Saxe-Coburg, an uncle of Britain's future Queen Victoria, was chosen as the first King of the Belgians. He introduced a remarkably progressive constitution, and under his rule Belgium returned to some of its former prosperity and grace, becoming the world's second-most important industrial power. But the continuing French–Flemish divide deepened with the rise of Flemish nationalism. The Dutch were also unhappy and invaded Belgium soon after Leopold's accession, and it was only with the help of Britain and France that William was finally forced to recognize Belgium's status as "an independent and perpetually neutral state" in the Treaty of London of 1839.

Leopold II succeeded his father in 1865. In many respects he carried on his work: commerce and transportation continued to develop, the Dutch language was officially recognized in 1886, the vote was extended to all male citizens in 1893, and a law passed in 1898 gave equal rights to the Flemish and Walloon communities. But Leopold is remembered chiefly for one thing: the Congo.

Leopold and the Congo

Leopold had backed the expeditions of the explorer Henry Morton Stanley to the Congo basin during the 1870s and saw colonial possessions as a key to Belgium's economic independence. Having made agreements with local African rulers and wormed support and money out of the European powers, he set up a confederation of states under his personal control. In effect, Leopold owned the Congo. Millions of Africans died, starved, or were mutilated in the service of his greed for rubber (for Belgium's new pneumatic tire industry) and ivory. The Congo generated vast revenue, but the appalling human cost of his colonial experiment eventually attracted international censure and in 1908 the Belgian state took control of the territory. The Congo finally became independent in 1960.

The Two World Wars

Germany's invasion of Belgium on August 4, 1914, in contempt of its neutrality, was one of the opening salvos of the First World War. Belgian losses were shocking: over 44,000 died and thousands were deported to Germany as forced laborers. Germany met accusations of barbarism with the retort that Belgium was not a real nation but an artificial construct with neither national traditions nor a strong government—but "plucky little Belgium" became a symbol of the beleaguered little nation crushed by the invader's arrogance.

Although Belgium received large reparations in the 1919 Treaty of Versailles, including what is now the German-speaking Eastern Cantons region and Rwanda–Burundi in Africa, the interwar years were harsh. Belgium endured the international economic crisis, a ruined infrastructure, and widespread poverty and hunger. A brief burst of political unity was soon shattered, ironically by the introduction of the "one man, one vote" system in the 1919 elections. This redrew the political landscape, making the Socialist Party, formed in the late nineteenth century, practically as strong as the ruling Catholic Party. The Catholics responded by edging leftward, becoming more Christian Democrat in their approach. Coalition governments became the norm. The 1930s saw unemployment and social unrest. In response to growing Flemish demands, the largely Walloon-biased government made Flanders and Wallonia monolingual regions in 1930, but left the linguistic boundary vague. Flemish nationalists and right-wing parties in Wallonia emerged, partly under the influence of fascist ideology, and made significant gains in the elections of 1936.

When the Second World War broke out, Belgium, the corridor between Germany and France, was again invaded, on May 10, 1940. After just eighteen days Leopold III capitulated, supported by much of the population but not by his government. The government fled to England and formed a government-in-exile, leaving occupied Belgium to be run by a German military administration and the Belgian civil service (which refused to cooperate in the deportation of Belgian Jews). As German occupation became harsher, resistance intensified.

Thousands of Belgian Jews were deported and sent to concentration camps, but many people risked their own lives to save Jewish children and give them new identities. Belgium was liberated by the Allies on September 3, 1944.

The Postwar Period (1945–70)
Immediately after the war, reprisals were taken against those who had collaborated with the Germans. Next, the question of Leopold's return caused political upheaval. He had spent the war under house arrest in his palace at Laeken, until freed by the Allies in 1945, when he went into exile. The referendum on his return split the country and caused the coalition government to collapse. A new parliament voted in 1950 to reinstate the king, but his return that year provoked such vehement protest, particularly among Walloon Socialists, that he was forced to abdicate in 1951 in favor of his son Baudouin I.

The postwar period was one of growth and recovery. Women gained full suffrage in 1948. The postwar governments were ready to make international alliances, and Belgium went from being the battleground of Europe to being its geopolitical crossroads. Belgium was one of the first countries to sign the U.N. Charter; in 1950 it joined NATO, and it played a formative role in what was to become the European Union.

Belgium Today

While Brussels has become the meeting point of European nations, its two major communities have drifted further apart. After the Second World War the economic fortunes of Flanders and Wallonia were reversed: in Wallonia mining declined and the steel industry was largely sold to foreign companies, while in Flanders new industrial sectors generated new wealth and confidence, accompanied by demands for linguistic parity. A linguistic frontier between French- and Flemish-speaking regions was drawn, not altogether successfully, in 1962, and between 1970 and 2001 government was progressively decentralized in a federal system in which the linguistic communities took over many powers.

In the 1990s Belgium looked comfortable, but was dogged by economic problems, disaffection with the main political parties, and, in 1996, the political embarrassment of an ugly scandal involving the abduction, rape, and murder of young girls by a pedophile, Marc Dutroux, in which alleged police collusion and inaction shocked people as badly as the crimes themselves. As King Albert II appealed for calm, Flemings and Walloons united in street protests.

At the 1999 parliamentary elections, a six-party Liberal–Socialist–Green coalition led by Guy Verhofstadt broke the Christian Democrat party's forty-year tenure of power. In the 2003 polls, the Greens lost their place in the governing coalition, which is now Liberal–Socialist.

THE LINGUISTIC DIVIDE

That Belgium is a country where two main languages, Flemish and French, are spoken is probably the first thing you will notice about it. Very soon afterward—possibly in a matter of minutes—you will realize that this linguistic duality determines a lot about Belgium, from daily social interaction to the way the country is run. In Belgium, language has always been an instrument of power, but as our overview of history has shown, linguistic dominance has ebbed and flowed on the tides of history without either side definitively "winning" once and for all. The result is a society where practically every institution is carefully duplicated along linguistic lines and where people on either side of the divide often profess to know nothing of each other's lives.

The story goes back to the Frankish period, when the Germanic Franconian language, the basis of modern Dutch, replaced Latin, the basis of French, throughout the Low Countries. By the Middle Ages, however, French was the established language of the nobility in Flanders, and until independence there was only one period (1815–30) when Dutch was the national language, and that by imposition. Dutch was not accepted as an official national language until over half a century after the creation of the Belgian state, and even afterward it was ridiculed as the language of peasants, not of polite society. Although a law passed in 1898 decreed that all legislation should be in both languages, the dominance of French was only really reversed in the twentieth century, as Flanders's economic and political clout began to outstrip Wallonia's and as Flemish demands for linguistic parity finally led to legislation giving Belgium's three major languages equal status and laying down, in 1962, a linguistic divide between the Dutch-speaking north and the French-speaking south, with a bilingual Brussels.

Dutch speakers now make up roughly 60 percent of the population and French speakers 40 percent. Brussels, though geographically in

Flanders, has a majority of French-speakers. German, the third national language, is spoken in the Eastern Cantons by about 70,000 people.

Enforcing linguistic parity can have bizarre results. People in public life must speak both major languages, and in a famous case in the mid-1980s the French-speaking mayor of Fourons (Voeren) in Limburg was disqualified because he refused to take the requisite Flemish examination.

Opinions differ as to whether the language of Flanders should be called Dutch or Flemish. Standard Dutch (*Algemeen Nederlands*) is the official language as taught in schools and used in institutions in both the Netherlands and Flanders and generally in literature. Within the spoken language there is considerable variation and a number of regional dialects.

There is a Bruxellois dialect, which incorporates Flemish words and Flemish-influenced syntax, but it is not often spoken to foreigners or identified by them, since the Bruxellois have learned to speak slowly and clearly to foreigners in French and often English. The old Walloon language is still spoken, though it is not officially recognized and is retreating in the face of French.

BELGIUM'S CITIES
Belgium is one of the world's most highly urbanized countries: 53 percent of its population

live in towns and cities. These, including Brussels, are mostly in Flanders, where the great towns of Ghent, Antwerp, and Bruges grew up in the Middle Ages, but there are also significant urban zones in the Wallonian industrial belt stretching from Mons to Liège.

Brussels

Brussels (Bruxelles in French, Brussel in Dutch) is Belgium's capital and the "capital" of the European Union. Its name derives from the Frankish Bruocsella, "village in the marshes." Its magnificent city hall, built in the fifteenth century, was almost the only building to survive the French bombardments of the town in 1695 and 1700. The famous Manneken Pis fountain, sculpted in 1619, which provided the district's water supply, also escaped destruction; its  cheeky charm, said to be symbolic of the sense of humor of the people of Brabant, also surely reminds us of their indomitability.

The Upper Town, around the Place Royale, survived 1695 but gradually morphed from a medieval to a neoclassical townscape during the eighteenth century. It contains several major museums and art galleries. After independence in 1830 many grandiose buildings were erected, especially by Leopold II, and magnificent central avenues and parks were created. Massive redevelopment in the thirty years following the Second World War, and the arrival of the European institutions, saw many of the boulevards and elegant residential districts swept away for fast bypass roads, tunnels, and vast office blocks. However, after years of neglect and unregulated property speculation, historic buildings are beginning to be restored.

Antwerp

Antwerp (Antwerpen/Anvers) is the largest city of Flanders and the capital of Antwerp province, with a population of around half a million. It is Belgium's second city and largest port, and the harbor is being extended right to the border with the Netherlands. The port has enabled the growth of other industries, such as petrochemicals, vehicles, and telecommunications. The city has long been the center of the world's diamond trade, and more recently has been put firmly on the international fashion map by a group of designers called the Antwerp Six. At the same time, the maze of narrow streets, passageways, and squares of the old city contain many fine buildings, Renaissance courtyards, baroque gardens, art galleries, and works of art. Here you will also find some of the most fashionable cafés and restaurants.

Antwerp is thought to be the most Dutch of the Flemish cities. It is not as fanatically neat and tidy as, say, Bruges; it has a larger-than-life air, a rather Italianate openness and warmth—some might say brash and assertive. It has significant African, Muslim, and Jewish communities, but in recent years has also become a stronghold of the openly racist and Flemish-separatist Vlaams Blok.

Bruges

Bruges (Brugge), the capital of West Flanders province, has a population of around 120,000. It is best known as the heart of tourism in Belgium. Having survived the two World Wars unscathed it has remained a medieval Flemish city, perfectly preserved with its cobbled lanes, canals and bridges, and exquisite buildings. Linked by a series of canals to Zeebrugge and Damme and to Sluis in the Netherlands, it is sometimes referred to as the Venice of the North and is usually as overrun with tourists as its namesake. Its museums and churches hold many of the country's fifteenth-century art treasures, and the city makes the most of its evocative beauty. But the same time-capsule quality that keeps Bruges economically alive also makes it something of a museum city. Bruges was placed on Unesco's World Heritage List in 2000.

Ghent

With a population of 224,000, Ghent (Gent, strictly speaking Gent-St-Pieters/Gand) is the capital of East Flanders. It has been an important inland port since the Middle Ages and is now Belgium's second port and a major industrial center, a shining example of Flanders's diversified economic renaissance. Nevertheless, it remains a town of medieval towers, crooked canals, and waterside gardens. The city has many Flemish Renaissance houses and guildhalls, a great cathedral housing the famous "Ghent altarpiece" by Jan and Hubert van Eyck (1432), and three *begijnhoven* (*béguinages*). The *begijnhof* was a peculiarly Flemish medieval institution—a quasi-religious community where single women could live and carry out good works, for instance as nurses, without entering convents. Ghent is also a university city with over 40,000 students, their bicycles filling the streets.

Liège

Liège (Luik in Dutch, Lüttich in German), the capital of Liège province, is situated at the confluence of the Meuse and Ourthe Rivers. With over 600,000 inhabitants, it is Belgium's third-largest city. Liège is the symbol of Belgian industrialization. The fighting spirit of its workers, derived from the city's adoption of the philosophy of the French Revolution, is legendary. The economic base took some hard knocks in the twentieth century, first from the two World Wars and then from the downturn in heavy industry, but Liège today boasts Europe's third-largest river port and is still the center of Belgium's small-arms manufacturing industry.

The first impression of Liège is of grim industrial and postindustrial sprawl, but its heart is charming, with several fine Romanesque churches. It has some outstanding museums and an elegant shopping district. Georges Simenon, creator of Inspector Maigret, was born in Liège.

Namur

Namur (Namen) is strategically situated at the confluence of the Sambre and Meuse Rivers and for most of its history was a military post. To this day the remains of its huge citadel dominate it.

The city has a population of just over 100,000; it is the capital of Namur province, the political capital of Wallonia, and seat of the Walloon parliament. Most of its medieval buildings have been destroyed, although much survives from the seventeenth and eighteenth centuries. Namur today is a peaceful place of narrow streets and tiny squares. One long-running tradition is the Académie des Quarante Molons (Academy of Forty Liars). They have elevated lying to a fine art and only the best liars of Namur qualify to join.

GOVERNMENT AND POLITICS

Belgium's form of government is a wonderful illustration of the unity-in-diversity that threads through the whole society, and at the same time of the "Belgian compromise"—the process of devolving some power to every stakeholder in a dispute, no matter how complex and even internally contradictory the result.

Belgium is a constitutional monarchy and a federal parliamentary democracy. The national-level parliament consists of a 150-member elected chamber of representatives and a 71-member senate (semi-elected). The monarch is the official head of

state and the prime minister is the head of government. The cabinet, or Council of Ministers, is appointed by the monarch and approved by the federal parliament, and must contain an equal number of French- and Flemish-speakers.

The central government is not very strong, however, and much practical power lies with the administrations and assemblies of the regions and communities, and even with local government at the level of the *commune* or *gemeente*.

A Complex System

Geographically, the country consists of ten provinces and the capital region of Brussels, but the bureaucratic picture is more complicated. Constitutional reforms created a federal political system with a three-tier form of government by dividing the country into three separate linguistic communities (Flanders, Wallonia, and the German-speaking Eastern Cantons) and three regions (Flanders, Wallonia, and Brussels), as well as the federal level of government. The regions and communities were granted economic and cultural competences, and there is now a complex division of federal and devolved responsibilities. Each region and community has an elected legislative assembly, making a total of six governments, each with its own legislature. The system is the best compromise found so far for keeping all the language communities happy, but it is so complex that there is a special Minister for Administrative Simplification.

With such a fragmented structure, Belgium's representative democracy is highly developed. Citizens have to vote for six or seven levels of government—the commune, the province, the regional and language community assemblies, the federal Chamber of Representatives and Senate, and the European Parliament. Voting is compulsory, too, although there is always some abstention. Federal elections are held every four years. The federal government elected in May 2003 is a Liberal–Socialist coalition of four parties, two

Francophone and two Flemish—for political parties, too, are constituted along linguistic lines. Of Belgium's nineteen parties very few operate as pan-Belgian parties, most—including the major parties—being either Flemish, Francophone, or German-speaking. Federal government policies have to benefit all language communities equally.

The Return of the Nationalist Right

Recent elections have reflected a growing alienation from traditional politics. In 1991 many voters in both language camps abandoned the Socialists, Liberals, and Christian Democrats for newer, smaller, issue-based parties, including Green parties. Perhaps the most visible recent trend in Belgian politics is the rise of the Flemish far right. In 1991 the Flemish nationalist Vlaams Blok (VB) startled the nation by capturing 25 percent of the vote in Antwerp; by the 2003 elections it had 30 percent, and about 20 percent of seats in the Flemish parliament. The VB, founded in 1978, calls for autonomy for Flanders (its on-line newsletter is called *Flemish Republic*) and the repatriation of foreign immigrants, and wants Brussels to revert to being a Flemish city. In 2004, after being condemned in court as a racist party, the VB reinvented itself as the Vlaams Belang ("Flemish Interest"), but the new party is scarcely distinguishable from the old.

THE ECONOMY

Despite its history of conflict and occupation, Belgium has had periods of outstanding prosperity: the "Golden Age" of the Renaissance, for instance, and the half century before the First World War. Around 1910, Belgium was the third-greatest commercial power in the world, its wealth based on railway infrastructure and rolling stock. The present day is showing signs of becoming another such period, as the economy develops and modernizes and the ever-growing presence of the European Union raises the country's profile.

The New Diversification

For centuries the fulcrum of Belgium's economy has shifted back and forth between south and north, Wallonia and Flanders. Currently, it is Flanders that is in the ascendant, with its highly diversified industry covering sectors such as textiles, paper, machinery, food processing, biotechnology, pharmaceuticals, telecoms, and horticulture, and, as ever, reaping the benefits of its great trading ports. However, recovering from the decay of its heavy industries, Wallonia too is restructuring its economy toward light and high-tech industry and services, assiduously aided by the region's authorities. Small-arms manufacturing is a long-established industry, and Saudi Arabia is currently a principal buyer.

At the national level, then, Belgium's economy is now principally dependent on services, transportation, manufacturing, and, of course, trade. Although its manufacturing industries depend heavily on imports, its exports are very high in relation to its size and population. Agriculture accounts for only a very small percentage (1.3 percent in 2001) of the gross domestic product and employs a correspondingly small percentage of the workforce (2 percent).

One of the highest taxation regimes in Europe, combined with the traditional Belgian scorn for regulations, has probably been behind the country's flourishing black economy.

Brussels, a Special Case

Meanwhile, Brussels has developed quite separately from either Wallonia or Flanders, because of its position as host to the European Union and a horde of international institutions and companies. Of course, this has been good for the whole country too: Belgium's chief trading relationship is with the E.U., to which it sends 75 percent of its exports. In Brussels itself, the presence of so many institutions—governmental, intergovernmental, nongovernmental, and commercial—has fueled the creation of a host of service industries, as well as a large construction industry. As much as the Bruxellois may grumble that incomers have pushed up the price of everything, Brussels has grown fat on this latest invasion. However, it is a polarized city, containing both the richest and the poorest districts in all Belgium, and has higher unemployment than either Flanders or Wallonia.

BELGIUM IN EUROPE

From being the "cockpit of Europe," Belgium has become its hub. Rising from the ashes of the Second World War, the governments-in-exile of Belgium, the Netherlands, and Luxembourg signed an agreement establishing the Benelux Customs Union in London in 1944. This came into force in 1948 and was followed a decade later by the Benelux Economic Union Treaty. Extending political and economic integration still further, in 1957 the three Benelux countries became founding members of the European Economic Community, now the European Union. Brussels is now home to the three key institutions of the E.U.—Council, Commission, and Parliament (though the Parliament also sits at Strasbourg)— and to many other pan-European organizations.

There is no denying that the E.U. has put Belgium, and particularly Brussels, back on the international map. Although the geographic center of the E.U. is moving steadily eastward with the accession of ten new states in 2004 and most other Eastern European countries lining up to join, Brussels remains the hub. The Belgians are divided on exactly how much of a good thing this is. The E.U. is undoubtedly a rich source of employment, but many Belgians—particularly Flemings—who work in Brussels refuse to live there, and commute daily. Many Flemings consider Brussels a Flemish city that has been co-opted by Francophones. There is some resentment of "Eurocrats," a feeling that the invaders don't contribute to the city's prosperity because they tend to live in foreign enclaves in the suburbs. But Belgian pragmatism and adaptability is such that Brussels is an easy city for foreigners to live in—small, with a good local transportation system, multilingual, and very cosmopolitan, with shops, restaurants, and entertainment catering to every taste.

BELGIUM IN THE WORLD

The exploitation of the Congo gave Belgium one of the worst imperialist records among European countries. However, although the slate can never be wiped clean, and the current state of the Congo basin countries is certainly in part a legacy of the colonial period, Belgium's participation in international affairs today is more benevolent. Former foreign minister Louis Michel, appointed a European Commissioner in 2004, has tried to atone for the colonial past by helping to reactivate the economy of the Democratic Republic of Congo and its neighbors Rwanda and Burundi and supporting the resolution of central Africa's ongoing conflicts. In 2002 he formally acknowledged Belgium's share of the moral responsibility for the killing in 1961 of Patrice Lumumba, the father of Congo's independence.

Belgium has been a member of the United Nations since 1945 and is a member of all the major U.N. institutions, as well as of NATO, whose headquarters is in Brussels. It participates in a number of U.N. peacekeeping operations, for instance in Afghanistan and in the Balkans.

Brussels, City of Lobbyists

More than a thousand international organizations are represented in Belgium, most with offices in Brussels, making it a magnet for political and business lobbyists. In recent years academic political think tanks have been joined by a horde of corporate-sponsored centers for policy research.

chapter two

VALUES &
ATTITUDES

"I love Belgium because it is there.
I hate Belgium because it is there."
(*Geert van Istendael*, The Belgian Labyrinth
[Het Belgisch Labyrint])

"*Et tant pis si je n'comprends pas / La moitié de ce
petit pays, / Je me sens partout chez moi /
Et je vous crie.*"
["And too bad if I don't understand /Half of this
little country, / I feel at home everywhere /
And I call to you."]
(*Song lyrics, Sandra Kim and Luc Steeno,*
"*J'aime mon pays*" ["*Ik hou van mijn land*"])

Two main factors seem to determine the values
Belgians hold and the ways they approach life: the
effects of the linguistic divide, and the country's
long history of exposure to other cultures through
trade, war, and occupation—its experience of
being simultaneously very small and very
strategically placed.

SEPARATE BUT NOT SEPARATE…

There are clear differences between the cultures of Flanders and Wallonia, but they are certainly not black and white. According to the strong regional stereotypes, the Flemish are more "Germanic" or northern European—reserved, puritanical, driven by the work ethic—while the Walloons are more "Latin" or southern European—gregarious, flamboyant *bons vivants*. Although they contain a grain of truth, such stereotypes are of course crude, and the reality is much more nuanced. Flemish Antwerp, like its baroque architecture, is Italianate and larger than life, and the city has a reputation for being permissive and raunchy. Ghent has always been bilingual, its upper classes speaking both French and the Ghent dialect (today a strongly accented Dutch), but it exhibits characteristics thought of as Flemish, such as a fierce independence. On the other hand, Francophone Namur and Mons, for instance, are both labeled dull, staid, and old-fashioned; the Liégeois combine gritty—some would say defiant—independence with cheerful vitality; and any attempt to pin language-related stereotypes on internationalized Brussels is doomed to failure. The picture is complicated yet further by the past and present movements of people within Belgium, and by immigration (see below).

Yet the language question is seen as the major

cultural determinant of the ways in which
Belgians understand and define themselves and
other Belgians. The very late acceptance of Dutch
as a national language—despite the fact that it
was, and is, the first language of well over half the
population—still rankles among Flemings;
Walloons, on the other hand, often think Flemings
make too much fuss about it. Neither community,
though, is particularly eager to use the other's
language: it is common to find Flemish people
who speak English, Spanish, or Arabic, but will
not use French, and Francophone public officials
reluctantly take adult education classes in Dutch
in order to fulfill the requirements of their jobs. In
both Flanders and Wallonia, school pupils choose
to study English rather than the other main
national language. The press and media, too, are
divided strictly by language. Yet Belgians from
both sides of the language divide love talking
about Belgium: what it is, how it works, whether it
works, why the differences, whether there will ever
be a complete split.

For all their differences, the language
communities share many values and
characteristics, and all three of them would rather
continue to be elements of Belgium than be
swallowed up by their historically more powerful
neighbors. Very few in either Flanders or Wallonia
would want their region to secede from Belgium

and join France or the Netherlands. Not even the tiny Eastern Cantons are interested in submerging their identity into that of Germany.

There are more positive unifying elements, too. The royal family is one, as a symbol as well as an institution. Religion is another. Both Flanders and Wallonia are strongly Catholic, though even here there are shades of difference. Catholicism tends to be more conservative in Flanders than in Wallonia, and their Catholicism is another distinction the Flemish draw between themselves and the historically Protestant Dutch.

Language and Class

For centuries French was the language of the ruling class, the various Flemish dialects spoken by the ruled. The Flemish dialects were despised even by the Flanders bourgeoisie, who tended to use French. The language divide no longer corresponds very closely with any class division, however. Once Wallonia became the center of the industrial working class and of a strong Socialist and labor movement, the use of French became more a badge of place. Today, Belgians do not make much of social class, though more conservatively minded people, mostly of the older generation, can be snobbish. In both language communities, social standing is based principally on wealth; the "old" families are mostly Walloon.

THE LEGACY OF OCCUPATION AND TRADE

Belgium has long been a meeting point of different cultures, languages, and forms of religion, both as a center of trade and, more traumatically, as an occupied territory. These things have helped mold the values and attitudes of today's Belgians: they tend to be cautious and avoid risks, but at the same time they have a strong antiauthoritarian, subversive streak. Having suffered in the past from fanaticism, as well as having long experience of dealings with other peoples, they are adaptable and tolerant. But they are perhaps also overmodest about their country's achievements and potential, critical of its failings, and self-deprecating personally and collectively.

"Ce Petit Pays"

This is a phrase used constantly by Belgians to describe their own country, even on government Web sites. Why do they insist so much on their country's smallness? Can the image of "plucky little Belgium" still apply in an age where the country is at the hub of the world's largest trading bloc? Given their history, one might expect Belgians to feel pride at having survived; perhaps the point is that Belgium has always *survived* the wars fought over it, rather than won them.

Belgians tend to be modest and unassuming as individuals and as a nation. There seems to be an assumption that the country is too small and powerless to undertake any bold enterprises. People are seldom anxious to impress others with their achievements, or to prove themselves in the right. Although Belgium is one of the world's greatest exporters, it has few internationally recognizable brands, except for Stella Artois, although beers such as Leffe and Hoegaarden are now making quiet inroads in Europe. Belgium is a world leader in vehicle manufacturing, but it hasn't had an automobile brand of its own since the 1930s and now hosts vehicle assembly plants for Ford, Volvo, Volkswagen, and other big brands.

Belgium did have some big brands in the early twentieth century, when there was a spirit of enterprise fueled by industrial strength and inventiveness, but these have mostly become internationalized. There are Belgian interests in many of today's multinational corporations, but they are not very visible. As Belgian financier Albert Frère said, "To live happily, we live hidden."

At the same time, without being self-promoting or ostentatious, Belgians are individualistic. Their personal style is outwardly quiet and low-key, but can hide Magrittean eccentricities: the suited gentleman you pass in the street may be a private collector of lawnmowers or nineteenth-century sex aids; odd museums lurk behind ordinary-looking doors; backstreets harbor shops selling bizarre clothes and jewelry, old comic books, or church pews. Individualism can also be seen in sports, where Belgians excel at solo sports such as tennis and cycling rather than team sports, and in architecture.

Antiauthoritarianism

The Belgian tendency to be skeptical of authority and unwilling to obey rules without question has roots in the country's having had so many externally imposed rulers and so little say in its own government—although it is also almost certainly a reaction to the multiple levels of bureaucracy generated by the multilingual system.

Belgians instinctively distrust any system that tells them what to do or how to think, and refuse to follow orders blindly. Whereas in the past antiauthoritarianism was expressed in insurrection, it tends to be expressed more mildly nowadays, in tax evasion (regarded by many as a national sport) and disregard for traffic rules and petty bureaucracy. There were a number of high-level scandals in the 1990s. More recently, a case of severe corporate mismanagement at Picanol led to the resignation of the company's CEO, Jan Coene, in October 2004, and to the drafting of legislation obliging companies to publish the salaries and other income of their top managers.

Scandals involving corrupt politicians and

donations to political parties are more frequent. In fact, when regulations on the financing of political parties did away with the informal system of political favors that existed from the 1950s to the 1970s, the result, especially in Flanders, was a sense of grievance at the loss of these opportunities rather than satisfaction at the achievement of political purity.

Political cynicism (some say apathy) is very widespread; it is generally assumed that politicians are corrupt. Despite their many opportunities to vote, Belgians' sense of public ownership of their several levels of government is weak. Ideology is seldom trusted: the Flemish far right is unusual in elevating its racist attitudes into an ideology.

THE GOOD LIFE

Anyone who has eaten a meal at a good Brussels restaurant will not be surprised to learn that Belgians are fond of creature comforts—good food and drink, spacious and well-furnished houses, leisure. This quality is not incompatible with hard work, but it does ensure avoidance of stress: Belgians value their evenings, weekends, and vacations, and know how to enjoy them (see Chapters 4 and 6). The much-traveled novelist Amélie Nothomb speaks affectionately of the "Pax Belgica" she finds at home in Belgium, by which she means restfulness, serenity, and comfort.

The desire for the good life seldom translates into the kind of ambition that seeks wealth for its own sake. Belgians hold a good work environment in higher regard than, for instance, good prospects for advancement in a job or even job security, and they tend not to change jobs very often, once they have found a job in which they feel happy.

Caution and Practicality

Although Belgians love the good things in life, it is very Belgian, and especially very Flemish, not to take risks, particularly with money. Flanders has the highest level of savings in the European Union. In Wallonia people are reputed to be more spendthrift.

This cautious attitude is linked to a firm pragmatism, a refusal to risk valuable benefits on a whim or for a "cause." Belgians prefer to make choices rationally, and this is one reason why both religious and political rigidity are anathema to them. Some see the recent development of the economy through diversification as evidence of this pragmatically minded adaptability.

Belgian practicality is reflected in art, too, by an interest in concrete details rather than abstraction. This can be seen in the work of the great fifteenth-century painters—think of the little dog or the carelessly thrust-off pair of shoes in Van Eyck's *Arnolfini Wedding*, Pieter Bruegel's earthy village scenes, or the Flemish talent for portraiture. In fact, the down-to-earth and the surreal can be two sides of the same coin, as we see in Magritte, whose surrealism consists in the subversive representation of everyday objects.

A TALENT FOR COMPROMISE

The tendency toward compromise rather than conflict is very Belgian. Belgians dislike confrontation and avoid taking extreme positions. Both the political system and industrial relations are based on compromise, where issues are resolved by conceding something to every stakeholder, even if the result is extremely complicated and often inefficient.

The treatment of the linguistic divide is the classic case of *le compromis belge*. However deep the differences between the two main language communities, since 1830 hardly anyone has died as a result of language-based political conflicts; disputes have been managed by peaceful demonstrations, public debate, negotiation, and legislation. The solutions may not be very elegant, but they do work. A frequent tactic is to avoid using any of the languages at all: thus piped music on Brussels's metro stations is either instrumental or in English, so as not to upset anyone.

Belgian labor relations also show compromise at work. These function through a system of negotiation between employers and workers, mediated by government and carried out at regular meetings, for instance to agree upon wage levels. There is an interesting historical background to this: in occupied Belgium during the Second World War, workers and employers abandoned their traditional opposition in order to sabotage production and to protect workers from being sent as forced laborers to Germany. Just before the Liberation in August 1944, trade unions and employers signed a "social solidarity" agreement; this has been further institutionalized, establishing the process of dialogue that shapes industrial relations in Belgium today. About 60 percent of Belgian workers belong to a union.

TOLERANCE

Belgian compromise is founded on a hard-won tolerance, a reaction, perhaps, against a past that contains so many examples of its opposite.

Attitudes to sex and death illustrate this clearly. Most Belgians are hard to shock and matter-of-fact about the body and its functions. Prostitution is open, though running a brothel is not actually legal. Jokes about sex, as in the 1995 film *The Sexual Life of the Belgians*, tend toward self-mockery. Belgium is the second country in the world after the Netherlands to legalize euthanasia. And it is now (after two years of heated parliamentary debate) perfectly legal to possess up to three grams of cannabis for one's own use.

As in much of Europe, Belgians marry later and divorce more often than in the past, and more couples live together before or without marriage. Divorce is generally accepted and is quite easy to get, though it is not taken lightly (after all, it represents a failure of compromise), and it is predictably rarer among practicing Catholics than others. Nonetheless, Belgium has the second-highest divorce rate in the E.U. (after the U.K.).

Homosexuality is officially accepted and same-sex couples, like heterosexual ones, can make their relationships official with a civil contract that establishes rights and obligations comparable to those of a married couple, including the disposition of property if the relationship breaks down or one of the partners dies. Belgium was the second European country after the Netherlands to recognize same-sex unions legally, in 2003. However, it is still illegal for same-sex couples to adopt children. The legal age of consent for gay men is sixteen.

. . . AND ITS BACKLASH

But tolerance can occasionally backfire, as in the shocking pedophilia case of 1996 (see page 34). Protests against the mishandling of the Dutroux case bloomed into an expression of general dissatisfaction with the incompetence and non-accountability of the justice system. More recently, a homophobic outburst by an octogenarian Belgian cardinal in early 2004 outraged many people, who regarded it as irresponsible particularly because, despite the advanced secularization of Belgian society, senior clergymen are still generally respected and heeded.

Organized racism, too, is a disturbing new trend. In 2004 the VB party used the sensitive issue of whether Muslim girls should be forbidden to wear the *hijab*, or headscarf, to school to stir up prejudice against Muslims (Belgium's second-largest religious group). Many find the growing popularity of the VB, with its extremist positions and racist language, not only morally repugnant but a very un-Belgian way of doing politics.

THE CATHOLIC HERITAGE

Belgium has no official religion, but the Church still has a strong influence in politics, business, and intellectual life in the Catholic universities.

The Catholic tradition has undoubtedly shaped

the mores of today's Belgium; but, even though the Belgian Church is relatively conservative, the influence and the practice of Catholicism are changing here, and for most people religion provides a moral and cultural environment rather than a set of rules or a guide for life.

Most people would call themselves Catholic, but it is estimated that fewer than 12 percent regularly attend Mass. A 1996 survey found 21 percent of Belgians defining themselves as "practicing believers," while 33 percent described themselves as "non-practicing believers." However, most children are still baptized and make their first communion. Church weddings are going out of style, though, and with noticeable differences between the linguistic communities: in Flanders, 51 percent of couples married in church in 1999/2000, in Wallonia 54 percent, and in Brussels, only around 20 percent.

MULTICULTURAL BELGIUM

Belgium has always been multicultural. For its whole recorded history its territory has been inhabited by more than one people. There has been internal migration and immigration. Not long after the Belgian nation was created in the nineteenth century, people flocked from poor

Flanders to newly industrialized Wallonia. Later, when coal production fell sharply during the Second World War, the employers' confederation recruited 77,000 Italian workers to the coal-mining areas of Hainaut and Limburg.

The population has become more mixed with the addition of immigrants from Spain, Portugal, Morocco, Turkey, Algeria, and Zaire. In 1999, 8.7 percent of the population was of foreign origin; this figure rose to nearly 30 percent in Brussels, which has significant Spanish and Portuguese communities as well as the expatriates brought by the E.U. and international organizations.

Especially in the Flemish cities, different ethnic groups tend to live side by side but not together—rather like the Belgian language communities themselves. Even in Brussels, ethnic minorities live in particular areas of the city. Ghent is an exception: here the immigrant population has become quite well integrated, owning shops and small businesses and speaking "standard" Dutch.

In fact, casual racism is quite common. It is risky to generalize, but the visitor to Belgium will soon notice that attitudes to non-European immigrants are different from attitudes to those from Western Europe. Central Africans, principally Congolese, are regarded more or less as part of the family, though not really equal to whites, because they are a responsibility inherited from the past. North Africans and Turks, even of the second and third generations, face much more racism. There has been an increase in the visibility of Islam recently, with women in Brussels seen wearing not just the *hijab* but the *burqa*; this has caused some uneasiness. On the positive side, Belgium appointed in 2004 its first regional state secretary from an ethnic minority community— Emir Kir, the son of Turkish immigrants.

MEN AND WOMEN

Officially, women have equality in Belgium, although they won the full vote and right to run for election only in 1948 and there are still very few women in high political office. Belgium's Catholic heritage must bear some responsibility for this. Abortion was legalized only in 1990, under bizarre circumstances: the devout (and childless) King Baudouin had himself declared "incapable of ruling" for a day in order to avoid ratifying the legislation.

Women's employment is high compared with some other Western European countries (40 percent of women are economically active), and women's equal work opportunities are promoted by good maternity leave provisions and ample day care for children from the age of two. Belgian men were in the forefront of lobbying the European Parliament

for flexible working arrangements in the 1980s.
Women's average wage is only about 45 percent of
men's, however. There is quite a lot of casual sexism,
and despite legislation against it passed since 1997,
domestic violence is still common and is both
underreported and underprosecuted.

ATTITUDES TO FOREIGNERS

Belgians are probably more tolerant of people
from neighboring Netherlands, France, or
Germany than they are of each other. The Flemish
consider the Dutch personally too assertive and
forthright and therefore a little intimidating, and
also absurdly obedient to their government; but
they are oddly fond of France, if chiefly as a place
to go on vacation. In fact, among Belgians
generally, France is the first choice for vacations.

Britain is another popular vacation destination,
although it has become much more expensive
post-euro. More people from Flanders visit Britain
than from Wallonia; according to one tourism
company, among the attractions is "British
eccentricity." There is some puzzlement as to why
the U.K. remains in the E.U., since its
commitment to the E.U. is considered poor and it
tends to side with the U.S.A. in foreign policy.

Many U.S. citizens live and work in Belgium,
especially Brussels, and many more visit as

tourists. The Iraq war and Belgium's adoption of legislation giving it jurisdiction over war crimes committed anywhere in the world have strained official relations between Belgium and the U.S.A., and some of this has rubbed off on Belgians' perceptions of Americans. However, antiwar demonstrators in Brussels in February 2003 told journalists that their anger was against the Bush administration, not Americans in general. Older Belgians still visit the American military cemeteries in Belgium in recognition of the U.S. Army's role in the Second World War.

ATTITUDE TO THE EUROPEAN UNION

Responses to the presence of the E.U. institutions, mostly in Brussels and its environs but also beyond, are ambivalent: they seem to have increased cosmopolitanism, but there is also some resentment that the country is being overrun yet again, this time by well-paid Eurocrats. Your first meetings with Belgians, therefore, may be tinged with reserve. It is sometimes hard to tell whether Belgians see the physically overwhelming E.U. buildings as a source of national pride or a symbol of the most recent invasion. Most people do not really know a great deal about how the E.U. institutions work in practice, even though they are right on the doorstep. At the same time,

"Eurosceptics" are rare, and there is some pride in this small country's place in the E.U. as a founding member. According to van Istendael, the way Belgium has managed its diversity with minimal conflict could be a model for Europe as a whole.

HUMOR: SITUATION DESPERATE, BUT NOT SERIOUS

It is always a delight to watch people encountering for the first time the surrealism that infuses so much of Belgian wit, art, and life—for instance, watching a television program by Les Snuls, a group of actors whose humor is based on wild satire of all aspects of Belgian life. Surrealism, as a movement, wasn't invented in Belgium, but you could be forgiven for thinking otherwise, so ubiquitous is it in Belgian culture. Even TV and

 cinema advertising veers toward the surreal. René Magritte (1898–1967) most famously illustrates Belgian surrealism, but as long ago as the sixteenth century, Hieronymus Bosch was painting apocalyptic but comical visions that can only be called surrealist. Today, surrealist wit is strong in the work of several Belgian artists, in cartoons such as Philippe Geluck's *Cat*, and—notoriously—in the exploits of Noël Godin, who has thrown custard pies at so many world celebrities that to be *entarté* ("flanned") by him is practically an honor.

Pie throwing, as political surrealism, shows the positive side of Belgians' deep-rooted skepticism about authority and rules and regulations. Comic strips, cartoons, and jokes have a strong anarchic flavor. You will find few superheroes in the classic Belgian comic strips—rather, ordinary folk with ordinary foibles will get caught up in weird and wonderful adventures and will often make complete fools of themselves. (See page 123 on comic strips.) Visual and physical humor are common, being more universally understandable than verbal wit. But there is also plenty of humor based on wordplay and linguistic inventiveness, which is not surprising in a country with three official languages and a host of still-living dialects. The exploration of language is a feature of both Francophone and Flemish literature.

At a less sophisticated level, Belgians often laugh at the expense of others. Several programs on Flemish television consist entirely of jokes in which Antwerpers, Limburgers, and West Flanders people cheerfully make fun of each other. Belgians are not necessarily happy, however, to recognize themselves in caricatures when the joke comes from outside. You should also be aware of the appropriate times and places to make ribald jokes and err on the side of caution.

SO ... IS THERE A NATIONAL IDENTITY?

Those who say Belgium doesn't really have a national identity often point out that it has no recognizable symbols (tulips, windmills, Alps, or cuckoo clocks). If symbols were all it needed, Belgium in fact has at least two—chocolates and beer—and a host of fictional or artistic signifiers in Tintin, the Smurfs, Maigret, Poirot, and the images of Magritte. More important representatives of the whole country are the royal family and Belgium's sports stars, past (the great cyclist Eddy Merckx) and present. Top tennis players Justine Hénin-Hardenne from Wallonia and Kim Clijsters from Flanders are an apt symbol of national unity *à la belge*: they both represent Belgium internationally, and are friends, but are equally loyal to their linguistic communities.

In the end, diversity itself is probably the truest image of the Belgian people. As we have seen, there is a degree of national identification, even if it is largely negative—not France, not Holland. But few Belgians would be happy just with the label "Belgian": they are also Flemish, Walloon, German-speaking, Bruxellois, or "new" (recently naturalized) Belgians. In fact, most people are more likely to identify with an even smaller unit, their city or province, and to define themselves first and foremost as Antwerpers, Liégeois, Limburgers, and so on. Pragmatic, unideological

Belgians love Belgium because it's a good place to live, but their primary identification is with the region, province, or town of their birth, where many of them will spend their whole lives.

And is there a Belgian national character? There are at least two. Again, we could define Belgians by the ways in which they are not like the French (less elegant, more practical/empirical) or the Dutch (less assertive, less Calvinist). But how to sum up the mixture of self-deprecation and love of the good life, the adaptability and the refusal to be led, the bland surface that hides subversion and quirkiness, the two communities forever on the brink of divorce but never actually splitting? The ensemble of contradictions that have been called *Belgitude* perhaps just goes to show that national stereotyping is an unreliable barometer—a conclusion that would appeal to most Belgians.

chapter three

FESTIVALS & CELEBRATIONS

Celebration is important to Belgians. The calendar bristles with festivals and local traditions. From local saints' days (*ducasses* or *kermessen*) to sea blessings, Mardi Gras to military commemorations, penitential processions to student rag days, a stream of extravagant festivals and folkloric events show Belgium at its most relaxed, and its most bizarre. Many ancient *fêtes* have hardly changed since the Middle Ages; others reflect legendary or historical events, and their pre-Christian origins often show through. Still others are quite recent and some are frankly tourist-oriented, but everywhere you will find the same tradition of grotesquerie and boisterous fun. Particularly at Carnival, few opportunities are lost to poke fun at authority figures and satirize politicians and other public figures. These are occasions that bring out the Belgians' anarchic streak, where reserve is abandoned and the love of good things and good fun reigns supreme.

PUBLIC HOLIDAYS

Ten public holidays (*jours fériés/openbare feestdagen*) are observed nationwide. Schools, banks, government offices, museums, and most businesses close on these days, although cinemas and restaurants remain open. If the day falls on a Sunday, the following day is the holiday. If it falls on a Tuesday or Thursday, many businesses have a four-day weekend, "making the bridge."

January 1: New Year's Day / *Le Jour de l'An / Nouvel An / Nieuwjaar*

March/April: Easter Monday / *Pâques / Paasmaandag*

May 1: Labor Day / *Fête du Travail / Feest van de Arbeid*

Early May: Ascension Day / *L'Ascension / Hemelvaart*

Seventh Monday after Easter: Whit Monday / *Le lundi de Pentecôte / Pinkstermaandag*

July 21: Belgian National Day / *Fête Nationale / Nationale Feestdag*

August 15: Feast of the Assumption / *L'Assomption / OLV Hemelvaart*

November 1: All Saints' Day / *La Toussaint / Allerheiligen*

November 11: Armistice Day / *L'Armistice / Wapenstilstand*

December 25: Christmas Day / *Noël / Kerstmis / Kerstdag*

There are also many regional and local holidays. Government offices and banks close on November 15, King's Day/*Fête de la Dynastie/Feest van de Dynastie*. Consult tourist information services.

A FESTIVE CALENDAR

The examples given below just scratch the surface of Belgium's festive calendar. Local tourist offices produce a calendar of the major events and listings can be found on www.visitbelgium.com.

January 6: Epiphany

This is the Feast of the Three Kings. In Flemish towns, children dress up as the Kings and call on houses, singing traditional songs and begging for sweets, fruit, or money. If these are given, the year and the initials of the kings, Caspar, Melchior, and Balthasar, are chalked on the front door to bring good luck over the coming year. Epiphany cakes, each containing a sweet or a tiny porcelain figure, are sold. Festivities continue with "Lost Monday"/ *Lundi Perdu/Verloren Maandag*, when traditional food is eaten in company.

February to April

The big festival of this period is Carnival/ *Carnaval*, which is celebrated everywhere around Mardi Gras, or Fat (Shrove) Tuesday, with costumes, pageants, and lots of things being thrown. At Binche, the highlight is the parade of the *Gilles*. Only men born in the town can wear the padded costume with its mask, ostrich-feather hat, and wooden clogs, and stomp around town to the beat of a drum, shaking bundles of sticks to ward off evil spirits and pelting onlookers with oranges. The oranges are blessings promising an abundant harvest—never throw one back.

Aalst's three-day carnival, beginning on the Sunday before Ash Wednesday, includes a parade of giants, the *Ajuinenworp* ("onion-throwing," though nowadays the onions are imitations), and the *Voil Jeannetten* ("dirty Janes"), an excuse for men in dresses and women in false beards to go around cheerfully insulting onlookers. Audience participation is unavoidable!

Ostend features a Procession of a Thousand Lamps and a fancy dress ball called the Dead Rats' Ball (*Bal des Rats Morts*). In mid-Lent, among the events in different towns is the march of the *Blancs Moussis*, in Stavelot, where men wearing white hooded garments and long red noses pass through the streets attacking spectators with confetti, dried herrings, and dried pigs' bladders. At Easter there is a fresh burst of dressing up and processing.

May

On May 1, or during May, a May Tree (*Meiboom*) is planted in some towns as a symbol of renewal. (In Brussels, surreally, they do it in August.) May 1 is also the *Fête des Muguets/Meiklokjesfeest*, an ancient spring rite in which bunches of lilies-of-the-valley are given as tokens of friendship.

The Holy Blood Procession (*Heilig-Bloedprocessie*) in Bruges, held on Ascension Day, is one of Europe's great religious pageants. The relic of Christ's blood brought to Bruges in 1149 by the Count of Flanders on return from the Crusades is paraded through the town in an elaborate medieval-style procession.

Less obviously Christian is the Festival of the Cats at Ypres on the second Sunday in May. Cats, the familiars of witches, were believed to personify evil spirits, and for 600-odd years from the twelfth century, live cats were thrown from the belfry of the Cloth Hall on this day. The event was revived in the 1930s, but more humanely—the cats are now toys. Every three years this festival culminates with the *Kattenstoet*, a parade of giant cats.

June to August

June 18 is the anniversary of the battle of Waterloo, celebrated every five years with a reenactment of the battle.

In June, many seaside towns stage annual Blessings of the Sea.

July 21 is Belgium's National Day, celebrated by a military parade in front of the royal palace in

Brussels, and firework displays countrywide. It is a public holiday, but is always rather upstaged by more picturesque celebrations, especially the Ghent Festival (*Gentse Feesten*), ten days of fireworks, outdoor music, street theater, fairs, and markets that take place around the National Day.

Early July is the time for the Ommegang ("walkabout") in Brussels, which recalls a procession held to honor Charles V in 1549, though it may date back to a fourteenth-century religious procession. The modern procession goes from the Grand Sablon to the Grand'Place, with participants in medieval costume, giants, and a battle fought on stilts. The climax is a traditional dance on the Grand'Place. Tickets for the finale need to be purchased well in advance.

Late August is rich in folkloric and historical celebration. The *ducasse* at Ath is another pageant featuring giants, this time in a wedding, and every five years Bruges honors the reign of the dukes of Burgundy with a Golden Tree Pageant.

September to December
The Sunday closest to September 8 in Tournai sees the Grande Procession of the relics of St. Eleuthère through the streets. This ceremony has taken place every year since 1092, after Bishop Radbod II vowed to hold a procession every year to thank the Blessed Virgin for relieving the city of plague.

Stilt fighting, much illustrated in tourist guidebooks, can be seen at its best at Namur in the Fight for the Golden Stilt (*Combat de l'Échasse d'Or*), where two teams of stilt walkers in medieval garb joust on the third Sunday in September as part of the Wallonia Festival.

The annual candlelit pilgrimage to Scherpenheuvel, Belgium's Lourdes and its most visited pilgrimage site, happens on the Sunday after All Saints' Day. According to legend, in the fourteenth century a miraculous statue of the Blessed Virgin was found in an oak tree (an image recalling a far older pagan worship), and the tiny statue is now housed in the town's baroque basilica. The popularity of the pilgrimage is a testimony to the strength of Flemish Catholicism.

On a more secular note, the students of Brussels's Free University (ULB/VUB) celebrate "Saint" Theodore Verhaegen, founder of Brussels's non-Catholic universities, in November. They rampage around demanding money in aid of charities and throwing eggs and flour over anyone who refuses.

"ORDINARY" FESTIVITIES

All these traditional and folkloric events jostle with food festivals, arts festivals (see Chapter 6), and occasions to make a party out of just about anything. Yet, in this crowded calendar, Belgians also find time somehow to celebrate Christmas, the New Year, Easter, and various family occasions.

Christmas/*Noël/Kerstmis/Kerstdag*

From early December, Christmas markets spring up in city squares and elaborate Nativity cribs appear in churches and museums; in some places, live farm animals are even part of the tableau. The day for giving presents to children is St. Nicholas's Day, December 6, not Christmas Day. Traditional presents include mandarins, chocolates, and models of the saint in *speculoos* (a spiced cookie made with brown sugar, cinnamon, and cloves).

But Belgium wouldn't be Belgium if there were not an exception to every rule. In the Waasland, northeast of Ghent, St. Martin performs the role of St. Nicholas, and the day is celebrated on November 11.

Everything closes down for both Christmas Eve and Christmas Day. Christmas Eve is very much a family event. Families have dinner together and may go to midnight Mass even if they are not regular churchgoers. Christmas Day continues to be family-dominated and is fairly low-key; there is another opportunity for Mass in the morning, after which families gather, exchange gifts (children get a few more presents), and eat a Christmas dinner featuring goose or turkey, sausages, and a Yule log cake.

New Year

On New Year's Eve (*Réveillon de Nouvel An/ Oudejaarsavond*—Flemings say good-bye to the old year rather than welcoming in the new) there is . . . more eating! This time people eat with friends rather than family and it is all much more gastronomically extravagant than Christmas; the dinner can continue through to dawn. The old year is sent packing with champagne and fireworks, and in Antwerp all the ships in the harbor sound their horns at midnight. On New Year's Day, traditionally children read out their New Year's resolutions to their grandparents or godparents before receiving a New Year's gift. It is traditional for this little ceremony to be sealed with a heart-shaped spiced bread.

Christmas and New Year cards are exchanged during the holiday season. If you receive cards from Belgian colleagues or friends, you should send one in return, ideally before January 15.

Easter

There is a charming story told to children about Easter eggs in Belgium. The legend has it that at the hour of Christ's death on Good Friday, all the church bells leave their belfries and fly to Rome. There they get Easter eggs from the Pope and set off home with them. By the morning of Easter Day they are back above their country, and as they return to their belfries they drop the Easter eggs into people's gardens, to be found, together with chocolate bells, by children. Why don't the eggs break? It's a miracle.

April Fool's Day

This is joyously and elaborately celebrated—don't believe all you read in the newspapers or see on television that day, and watch out for paper fish stuck on your back.

All Saints and All Souls

Halloween is not a Belgian tradition, but British and American influence means you will see jack-o'-lanterns, witches, and ghosts around, particularly in shops. Much more happens on All Saints' Day, when people bring chrysanthemums and candles to the graves of their dead relatives, and November 2, the Day of the Dead, when soul cakes are eaten to save souls from Purgatory.

WEDDINGS AND OTHER RITES OF PASSAGE

Only about half of all marriages now have a church ceremony. The civil ceremony, which is legally obligatory, takes place in the *maison communale* (town hall) and is followed by the religious ceremony, if there is one.

The wedding day generally falls into three parts: the ceremony, a reception in the afternoon, and a larger party at night. Many Belgians like to hold the wedding party in a château, and fortunately Belgium has plenty of these furnished with restaurants—the main problem is actually getting a date when the place is free.

If you are invited to a wedding, the invitation will make it clear whether you are invited to the church ceremony (only family attend civil ceremonies) and the following reception or dinner, or just to the party. Always acknowledge the invitation in writing. Wedding gifts are given, of course, and there is almost certain to be a gift list (*liste de marriage/huwelijkslijst*) from which you can choose a gift. You can either bring the gift to the wedding or have it sent to the bride's house before the wedding.

Fairly similar rules of etiquette apply to other occasions such as baptisms, first communions, or birthday celebrations—acknowledge the invitation with the same degree of formality with which it was issued, and bring a gift. Godparents are responsible for distributing *dragées* (sugared almonds) as mementos of baptisms. The guests offer presents, usually of clothes for the baby, but increasingly parents are drawing up "baptism lists" like wedding lists in a store.

Finally, funerals. Deaths and funeral dates are announced in the local newspaper, and you may receive a personal invitation to the funeral, to which you must reply. There is usually a viewing at the deceased person's home or a chapel in the hospice or hospital where they have died. Most Belgians still opt for a religious burial service, although the number of cremations is rising steadily. The service is usually followed by a light repast, to which you should go only if specifically invited. You can send flowers on the day of the funeral unless the announcement specifies no flowers.

DAILY LIFE

QUALITY OF LIFE

Belgium is a highly urbanized and generally affluent country, and nowadays that affluence is

spread fairly evenly, although there is still some poverty. Judged by unemployment levels and net income levels, Flanders is the most prosperous region, Brussels the poorest. Up to two-thirds of the poor are women. Belgium has an excellent social security system, with higher levels than either the U.S. or the U.K. of social protection such as unemployment benefits, maternity and sick leave benefits, and pensions. Taxation and social security payments are correspondingly high.

The crime rate is low: fewer than ten crimes per 1,000 inhabitants are reported per month. Burglary, robbery, car theft, and violent crimes are infrequent; domestic violence, though, is severely underreported, and the Dutroux case of 1996 has raised fears about children's safety.

HEALTH CARE

The health care system is one of the best in Europe and is also rather complex, with numerous health insurers (*mutualités/ziekenfondsen*) enabling you to recover most medical, dental, and other health care costs. To obtain these benefits, all employees of Belgian companies and self-employed people must join a health insurance scheme. A percentage of the employee's salary is deducted from the paycheck, and the benefits apply to both the employee and his or her dependents. Waiting lists for hospital treatment are almost unknown. At least partly because of this efficient system, Belgians have no qualms about calling the doctor. Doctors tend to prescribe readily, and many medicines can be bought over the counter. Herbal remedies are also popular.

Disability

Belgian law protects disabled people from discrimination in employment, education, and public service provision. Assistance for the disabled (provided by different levels of government) includes grants, and regional and community job training programs. Disabled people are eligible to receive services anywhere, irrespective of their region of residence.

Public buildings erected since 1970 should by law be accessible to the disabled, and government subsidies are available to the owners of older buildings to make their premises accessible; many buildings do not meet accessibility standards, however. Public transportation is not particularly disability-friendly, either.

FAMILY LIFE
In a small country where no one moves house much, family members are always in touch with one another and it is hard to get away from your family even if you want to. It is very typical for Belgians to visit their parents, grandparents, or in-laws once a week, and most see this as an obligation, not an option. Family relations are therefore close—sometimes too close for comfort.

Children
Like much of northern Europe, Belgium is not a very child-centered society. The birthrate is declining as people marry or settle down later in life, fewer people want children, and it is more socially acceptable for couples either to delay starting a family until their careers are established or to decide not to have children at all. Belgium's excellent preschool child-care provisions are conceived more as a way of facilitating women's employment than as an exercise in early learning for children.

However, those who do choose to have children are devoted parents and much of their lives revolves around the children and their development. Among the younger generation, fathers are taking a much more active role in child care than their own fathers did. Many families still observe traditional rites of passage. Children are usually baptized in the Church, and most make their first communion, though the ceremony is nowadays more an occasion for celebration and gift giving than an expression of devotion. At sixteen, schoolchildren are either confirmed, renewing the baptismal vows, or have a secular celebration.

The Third Age

Like most of the "developed" world, where birthrates are low and health services advanced, Belgium has an aging population. Life expectancy is seventy-five for men, eighty-one for women. The official retirement age is sixty-five, but not many people work that long, many choosing to retire as early as fifty. This entails quite a high cost to the government; increasingly, pensions take up more of GDP than health care does, and the trend is set to continue.

Belgians may choose to leave the economically active population as soon as possible, but once they've done so they remain extremely busy, taking classes, doing DIY, gardening, traveling. People also tend to continue living in their own homes until an advanced age—two-thirds of Belgians over eighty still do so—although rest homes are available.

EDUCATION

The Belgian schooling system involves twelve years of compulsory primary and secondary schooling between the ages of six and eighteen. However, nearly all children enter the education system at about two-and-a-half to three years old, attending an *école maternelle/kleuterschool*. Working parents of children under three can use the local crèche (*kribbe*) or day care, but because it is relatively cheap there is always a long waiting list. Even at this early stage the language divide makes itself felt, since different schools at all levels are run in different languages.

The administration of education rests with the language communities. Official state schools are directly financed by the state and follow the state curriculum exactly; the provinces and communes also organize schools, which approach the state curriculum more flexibly. Independent (mostly church-based) schools get some state funding, but parents may have to pay for some facilities. There are also private schools and a number of international schools. State-funded special schools are provided for children with serious learning difficulties or physical disability.

State education is now secular, but there is also an independent school network that is largely Catholic. Many families opt for an independent school, though not necessarily for religious reasons: they are also likely to choose a particular school because it is nearer their home or has a better reputation. In Wallonia, about half of both primary and secondary pupils go to state schools, but in Flanders the figure is only about 30 percent. The state system includes alternative educational methods such as Montessori, Freinet, and De Croly. Freedom of choice of education is constitutionally guaranteed, and schools cannot turn down an application without an objective reason, such as lack of places.

At around ten or eleven children start to learn a second language, usually the other national language, or English. Flemish children think English both easier and more "cool" than French. Walloon children, offered English, German, or Dutch, also tend to choose English; if they learn Dutch it will be their third language.

Nearly 80 percent of young people in Belgium have a diploma of secondary education from a

general, technical, or vocational secondary school.
The final exams qualify students for higher
studies, the certificate being valid in Belgium and
some other E.U. countries. Students can go to a
university or a further education college, and
nearly 60 percent of them do so. Most students go
home on weekends, and the trains on Friday
afternoons are full of young people carrying
bulging rucksacks. Access to lifelong learning is
open in all communities.

At eighteen Belgians reach legal age and can
vote, drive, marry, or start up a business. The
official age of sexual consent is sixteen for both
sexes, and by the age of seventeen, 50–60 percent
of Belgians have had their first sexual experience.

THE HOME AND HOMEMAKING

Belgians are very attached to their homes and
hometowns. They tend not to move frequently,
and often live in the same city or village for their
whole lives. This is possible because Belgium is so
compact and has such an efficient transportation
system that people do not need to relocate for
work but can commute.

As it happens, the railway system owes its
efficiency to policies designed precisely to keep
people living in their home areas. The railway
network was put together by a staunchly Catholic

government that wanted people to stay in their home villages and not migrate to the cities, where they might be won over to Socialism by trade unions or fall under the spell of other urban enticements. Thus, as the cities inexorably developed as centers of employment, a comprehensive network of rail links was built, so that practically everyone could commute—and they do. Every weekday afternoon thousands of Brussels workers flee the capital for towns as far away as Liège or Hasselt. Home is a status symbol, a hobby, and a refuge.

Patterns of Home Ownership

More than 60 percent of people own their homes, except in Brussels where the figure is neatly reversed and over 60 percent rent, the difference being largely due to the high proportion of foreigners living, often temporarily, in Brussels. For young Belgians, renting is seen as a temporary solution until they can afford to buy or build.

The presence of large numbers of foreign professionals has done much to promote the growth of the suburbs of Brussels and the villages around it, at the expense of the city center. Brussels-based expatriates tend to prefer the periphery, particularly if they have families and want more space than an apartment, and an international school for their children to attend. On the other hand, many MEPs (members of the European Parliament) own or rent apartments in the more affluent parts of the city center, which they occupy only part-time. Some residential areas of central Brussels are economically depressed, but this means that apartments in these city communes, often in stunningly beautiful buildings, can be very affordable. St. Gilles, for instance, has become fashionable, judging by its boutiques, restaurants, and food shops.

Few Belgians possess second homes: fewer than 3 percent have a second home in Belgium, and fewer than 1 percent have one elsewhere.

Buying and Renting

Buying a house or apartment in Belgium is expensive and time-consuming. House prices look temptingly low, but taxes and fees are high and processes are slow.

Homes for rent are of particular interest to expatriates. In Brussels especially, their preference for beautiful old houses with high ceilings and art nouveau or art deco decoration has contributed to the cessation of unregulated and speculative development. Such houses, or apartments in them, can be found particularly in Etterbeek, St. Gilles,

and other nineteenth- and early twentieth-century residential areas. Homes in the old quarters can be found in other main cities, too.

The rental system is quite complex. Houses and apartments are rented unfurnished (*non-meublé/ niet gemeubeld*) or furnished (*meublé/gemeubeld*). "Unfurnished" usually means that the property is let without light fixtures (expect bare wires sticking out of the ceilings), curtains or curtain rails, carpets, built-in storage, stove, or refrigerator. Furnished housing is more reassuring: it usually includes everything down to kitchen and dining ware, but probably not bedding or towels.

You may be taken aback by the number of rules and regulations applying to life in an apartment complex, referring to late-night noise, pets, garbage, use of elevators, and so on. You may subsequently be surprised at the extent to which these are flouted, offering you a great opportunity for practicing your skills in Belgian compromise.

Building One's Own

It's an old adage that "every Belgian is born with a brick in his belly," referring to the national preference for building one's own home. In Belgium you will hardly ever see a housing estate consisting of identical buildings, and even in city terraces each house will be different from its neighbor. This architectural individualism goes back quite a long way, as you can see from the exuberant variety in Brussels's streets, art nouveau treasures cheerfully rubbing shoulders with dour modernist apartment complexes.

As families get smaller and dwellings get more numerous, housing is taking up more and more space in Belgium. Belgians are increasingly choosing to live within easy access of green spaces and in environments they consider safer than the inner cities, so there has been a steady migration out of the cities since the late 1980s, particularly among young families with children. Besides putting ecological pressure on the countryside, this trend increases the gap between richer households in the green peripheries and poorer ones in the densely populated old centers. Planning regulations now limit nonagricultural building in rural zones and reduce the amount of land available for building. The legislation has put a brake on new building, and the focus— supported by tax incentives—has turned to the extension and renovation of existing buildings.

Lining the Nest

Once the house is built, it must be furnished. In general, homeliness—in the sense of loving one's home and enjoying tending it—is characteristic everywhere, but particularly in Flanders. Belgian houses tend to be comfortably furnished. The rather overstuffed and often dark-toned interiors favored by the older generation are giving way to a lighter and sparer style. Furniture stores are the new Sunday temples, Ikea leading the Belgian furniture market by a good margin. DIY is a national pastime. Once the children have grown and gone, many middle-aged Belgians spend time and money on doing up the house and garden.

THE DAILY ROUND

Belgians live, on average, 11 miles (17 km) from their workplaces. In 1999/2000, about 220,000 people from Flanders and about 116,000 from Wallonia were traveling daily to work in Brussels.

The working day starts as early as 8:00–8:30 a.m. and can often finish by 5:00 p.m., so people can get home before the evening rush hour—a rather self-defeating move, since it simply extends the rush hour. The working day at local government offices in particular starts and ends early. Lunch is taken with colleagues (either in or outside the office), and the cultivation of a pleasant working environment and friendly relations with colleagues is considered very important. After work people without responsibility for children may have a drink before going home, especially in the summer when it is so pleasant to spend half an hour at a sunny pavement café, but this isn't a daily fixture. Those with families will have a beer or two at home after dinner and children's bedtime.

A charming custom in Belgian workplaces is the reception. All kinds of opportunities, such as a birthday, are taken for staff to gather together in the office around lunchtime and indulge in wine, beer, and snacks. This is all part of building a harmonious work culture and good relationships between colleagues, and is very civilized.

The school day is from 8:00 a.m. to 4:00 p.m., though it is possible to drop children off any time after 7:00 a.m. and collect them up to 6:00 p.m. Parents (mostly mothers) spend much of the afternoon ferrying children between school, home, and after-school activities—sports, hobbies, visiting friends. Particularly since the Dutroux case, concern about children's safety has grown, so children are seldom left to make their own way about towns or even villages.

Then there is food shopping. Belgium's main supermarkets have branches everywhere, but it is more interesting to explore local bakeries and *pâtisseries*, *traiteurs* (delicatessens), tea and coffee specialists, wine merchants, and cheese stores (sometimes wine and cheese are in the same shop) in your neighborhood. Belgians do not share the

British obsession with waiting in line, so—although Belgians are far too polite to push in—take care not to lose your place in supermarket lines or shops that still use the numbered-ticket system. Some supermarkets have introduced handheld scanners that enable you to compile your own bill and save time by using special checkout lanes.

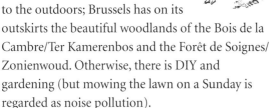

Weekends are devoted to keeping up family relationships, with family visits often combined with a walk or cycle ride. Even city dwellers take to the outdoors; Brussels has on its outskirts the beautiful woodlands of the Bois de la Cambre/Ter Kamerenbos and the Forêt de Soignes/Zonienwoud. Otherwise, there is DIY and gardening (but mowing the lawn on a Sunday is regarded as noise pollution).

PETS

One in every four Belgian households has a dog, and one in four a cat. That's more pets than the Dutch, the Germans, or the British. People tend to take their dogs everywhere, even into restaurants, which can be unnerving for British and American visitors. Pet care services and boarding kennels are abundant. Registering pets for identification is compulsory.

chapter five

MAKING FRIENDS

Socially speaking, you could describe Belgians as "sociable but reserved." They are more reserved than most North Americans, and less reserved than most Britons. This is of course a huge generalization, and you will find many younger or more cosmopolitan people who are less formal in their social relations; but if you operate on the basis that most Belgians will be friendly, kind, and helpful, and generously tactful about your language deficiencies, but not over-effusive or inclined to encourage familiarity in the early stages of acquaintance, you will not go far wrong. In particular—not unsurprisingly in a small, densely populated country—Belgians value privacy, especially at home, and have discovered that this is easiest to preserve without friction if personal relationships outside the family are well managed and social life is planned rather than impromptu. Most guides to etiquette in Belgium stress that you should not drop in unannounced on a Belgian

acquaintance or friend, even quite a close one—
always telephone first.

Most of your social contacts with Belgians,
therefore, will probably happen in public spaces.
The home is seen as the preserve of family life, and
much socializing with friends is done outside it. If
you are invited to dinner in someone's home
(most likely to happen in Flanders), the occasion
may in fact be quite formal, and it will not
necessarily be the overture to a closer friendship,
but may rather be intended to facilitate your stay
by introducing you formally to other people. It
will then be up to you to reciprocate by inviting
them in return, perhaps to a restaurant or a
cultural event (see below).

HOW NOT TO BE AN EXPAT

If you are working for a short time in Belgium or
making a business trip, you will of course meet
Belgians in the course of your work, but these
relationships are basically formal, at least in the
early stages. If you really want to immerse yourself
in Belgian life and culture, a good—though
bold—strategy is to resist the temptation to stay in
areas swarming with foreigners. The outer suburbs
of Brussels, such as Uccle, Woluwe-St-Pierre, or
Tervuren, are comfortable and user-friendly for
English-speakers, but they are expat enclaves and

by basing yourself there you could miss out on many of the fascinating nuances of living—even if only for a short time—in a more local environment. Although there is undeniably more to do in the big cities than in the villages, try to spend some time in the countryside, even if you just go for the weekend or take a short farm-based vacation (see Chapter 7, page 139).

Depending on the length of time you intend to stay, there are many ways you can experience the delights Belgium has to offer just as Belgians do—in off-the-beaten-track restaurants, bars, and cafés, in evening classes and interest groups, in sporting and outdoor activities, even soaking up the atmosphere in street markets.

It would be foolish to pretend, however, that when living abroad you need never take time out to speak your own language and relax with people of your own culture. Fortunately the expatriate community in Belgium is so large and well-established that this is easy to do. If you are staying in Belgium for some time, there are dozens of organizations in the English-speaking community, from nationality-based groups to amateur dramatic, music, and dance groups. In quite a number of these groups you will find Belgians too, honing their English skills. For upcoming English-speaking events, there is a column in the weekly *Bulletin* called "Happenings."

BEING A FOREIGN STUDENT

Belgian universities actively set out to attract international students, and all the main universities (Antwerp, Brussels, Ghent, Leuven, Louvain-la-Neuve, and Liège) participate in exchange programs with other European universities via the Socrates program and with universities worldwide via Erasmus Mundus.

There can be few better ways to get to know like-minded Belgians than this. Erasmus has a student network with sections in universities all over Europe whose job is to advise and support international students and organize social and cultural activities to help them integrate into student life. All the Belgian universities have a kaleidoscopic array of student societies, plus centers and services for international students.

JOINING CLUBS, SOCIETIES, AND CLASSES

In Belgium, they say that if three people come together in one place with a common interest or belief, they will form a society. There is an organized group for practically any activity you can mention. In Flanders alone, more than half the population are active members of at least one club or society. Even young adults with a full-time job and small children somehow manage to squeeze in several evenings a week to study the guitar, sing, act, play squash or football, learn a new language, practice salsa dancing, make pottery, or go to a political, environmental, or other interest group. So, if you're a "joiner" at heart, there are plenty of outlets for your sociability and opportunities to meet like-minded Belgians. You will need to be fairly proficient in French or Dutch, though, to take part fully, unless you join a club for expatriates—which would defeat the object of meeting Belgians.

Language Classes

Paradoxically, language classes, particularly in Dutch, are quite good places to meet Belgians, since many Walloons, having gone through the school system avoiding Dutch, find that they need both national languages for a job and have to take a crash course in Dutch. Learning a language that is not one of Belgium's national languages will of course bring you into contact with Belgians who are doing the same thing.

CAFÉ CULTURE

If all this talk of organized activity is making you tired, you may prefer to meet Belgians just by hanging out. You'll notice that the tables at cafés in Belgium are always full, at practically any time of day. Just sitting on a café terrace in the sun nursing a coffee—or, later on, a beer—you can rub shoulders with all sorts of people: suited businessmen in earnest, money-laden discussion, elderly ladies-who-lunch with big hair and infinitesimal dogs, excitable or exhausted tourists, and in the early evening, shoals of young workers disgorged from their offices. The atmosphere is always convivial but seldom raucous, even quite late at night. Belgians' love of café society is a delightfully Latin trait, but they don't tend to shout, guffaw, or wave their arms about extravagantly, so you shouldn't either.

If you have the self-confidence to start up conversations with people in bars, you should explore Le Pain Quotidien, a "concept" lunch place with several branches in Brussels and others in Leuven, Antwerp, Bruges, Liège, and Namur. The concept in question is that each Pain Quotidien is furnished with just one huge central table around which everyone sits. You don't *have* to talk to your neighbors at the table—plenty of lunchers bring their newspaper or a book—but no one will think you're crazy if you do.

Later at night, bars, some with live music, are open till the early hours. There are lively club scenes in Brussels, Antwerp, and other large towns.

HOSPITALITY

On the whole, particularly with people you don't know very well, social events like dinner parties tend to bring out the conservative rather than the anarchic side of the Belgian character. At least, it is a good idea to assume so until you discover otherwise. Obviously, as you get to know people better, you will be able to judge the level of informality with which you both feel comfortable.

Dinner Parties

If you are invited to dinner at a Belgian home, you should treat it as a fairly formal occasion unless you're specifically told that it will be super-informal. If you have received a written invitation, reply in kind, unless it is just a reminder of an invitation already made and accepted verbally—in which case the invitation may be marked "PM" (*pour mémoire*). "RSVP" ("VGA" in Dutch: *verzoek graag antwoord*) in the invitation demands a reply. Dress nicely (don't wear jeans, even if they're by Armani), be punctual (neither too late nor too early), bring a small gift for your hosts, don't overstay your welcome, and in general take your cue for behavior from your hosts and Belgian guests. Here are a few little rules to observe at the dinner table (they apply to meals in a restaurant, too, though behavior there may be more or less formal according to the kind of restaurant it is).

POINTS OF ETIQUETTE

- Wait to be offered a seat at the table by your host before sitting down.
- It is not considered genteel to leave food uneaten; in fact, it might be taken as a sign that you didn't like something. Make a point of complimenting your host on the food (it shouldn't be hard to do this with utter sincerity!).
- Avoid the American custom of cutting up your food with fork and knife and then eating it using only your fork in your dominant hand.
- When you have finished eating, place knife and fork neatly side by side on the plate.
- Follow your host's lead if toasts are given, and be careful not to drain your glass at the first toast in case there are others. There is usually a toast at a formal dinner, and you should not taste your wine before the host has led the toast.

Sometimes, gender relations you might regard as rather old-fashioned become evident, if the gathering is not seated around a table—at a cocktail party, say. You might arrive with a companion of the opposite sex and begin the evening in a mixed group, but before long the gathering will have divided into single-sex groups, with men on one side of the room, women the other. This rather Latin habit is more noticeable in Walloon than Flemish gatherings.

If you want to return the compliment of a dinner party but are not living in Belgium, it is perfectly acceptable to invite people to dinner in a restaurant or to a cultural evening, for instance at the opera or ballet.

If you are resident and are hosting a dinner party of your own, you can set the level of formality, but your Belgian guests will probably expect much the same rules to apply. Especially if the event is quite formal, you will need to seat people at the table: the usual seating arrangements place the host at the head of the table with his or her spouse (if present) opposite and the guest of honor of the opposite sex sitting on his or her right. This may sound Byzantine, but it saves the potential confusion and embarrassment of people not knowing where to sit.

Dress Codes

For social occasions, including visits to Belgian homes, the "smart casual" dress code is usually appropriate. Be aware, though, that Belgians tend to dress conservatively, so this tends toward the "smart" end of the spectrum. For men, a casual wool jacket and trousers or a linen jacket and well-cut chinos would be fine; for women, a shirt or blouse, trousers, and jacket, or in summer an elegant dress. Belgian women's clothes can be a little drab and unadventurously "classic," though well-made—not everyone can afford the great Antwerp designers. The important thing, though, is to keep your T-shirts, jeans, and sneakers for home, outdoor pursuits, and shopping.

Gifts

It's safe to say that you should never arrive empty-handed at any kind of event at a Belgian home. Flowers, a small decorative houseplant, chocolates, wine—all are suitable gifts for your host or hostess and will be accepted graciously. If you're coming straight from your own country or your visit is very short, a small gift from your country (an unusual whiskey, say) is also a good idea. In Belgium, gifts are opened in front of the giver.

A few things you should know about flowers: don't give chrysanthemums (they symbolize death), lilies (which have religious associations), or red roses (sexual love); and don't give thirteen of anything.

CONVERSATIONAL DOS AND DON'TS

• Don't discuss personal matters unless your Belgian interlocutor brings them up. The standard icebreaker, "And what do you do?" is unlikely to provoke a rush of talk.

• Don't talk about yourself too much either, although you can probably make a gentle joke or two at your own expense—it is quite a Belgian thing to do. Be modest about your own successes and accomplishments, as Belgians are about theirs.

• Dining is first and foremost a social occasion, so if you are dining with a colleague or client, don't talk business unless the host raises the subject. At a dinner party where spouses and partners are present, you will usually find business matters are not mentioned.

• It is tactless to talk about the linguistic and cultural divide, and you're on shaky ground asking even genuine questions about Belgian history or politics, unless your Belgian companions raise the subjects themselves.

• The E.U. is not a taboo subject, however, nor is travel in other countries. You can talk about your country, too—in moderation.

• Aspects of their country that Belgians will always discuss happily are food and drink (especially Belgian specialties), and both high and popular culture.

Topics of Conversation

It is difficult to give advice as to what you should and shouldn't talk about with anybody. Naturally, with Belgian friends you know well, the boundaries of acceptable conversation will have been established and adjusted as the friendship has developed. The points opposite refer to conversations you may have with people with whom you are not closely acquainted, at a stage of your acquaintance with Belgium when you might risk making a gaffe.

Thank-you Notes

Always remember to send a handwritten thank-you note to your hosts after being invited to any occasion, as soon as possible after the event. This could be accompanied with flowers, if you did not bring them to the event as a gift, or a basket of fruit.

TIME OUT

SHOPPING

Shopping in Belgium can be a delight, offering everything from fashion boutiques and large department stores to small neighborhood shops and open-air markets. Belgians themselves consider Antwerp the favorite city for shopping, combining avant-garde designer boutiques and one of Europe's ten biggest shopping malls with

secondhand shops and antique dealers—not to mention diamond dealers— tucked away in quaint cobbled lanes. In Brussels, key shopping areas are the Avenue Louise and Toison d'Or area and the indoor Anspach center at De Brouckere. The Galeries Royales St.-Hubert/ St. Hubertus Galerijen is a beautiful glass-roofed shopping arcade not far from the central station and the Grand'Place, built in 1847 and the first of its type in Europe.

A Chocaholic's Paradise

Belgium produces what many regard as the best chocolates in the world. Every town has at least two or three specialty chocolate shops, and the major cities have dozens. The main manufacturer/exporters are Godiva, Leonidas, and Neuhaus, but the Belgians keep the best for themselves, preferring Mary's, official purveyor of chocolates to the royals. Chocolates are sold by weight and you can make a selection for your kilo or half-kilo box or ask for a mixture (*mélange/mengsel*).

Opening Hours

Opening hours in the cities are usually 9:30 or 10:00 a.m. to 6:00 or 7:00 p.m. from Monday to Saturday, without a lunch break. Many shops have extended hours on Friday evening, and shopping malls tend to stay open longer in the evenings, to 7:00 or 8:00 p.m. Some smaller shops are closed on Monday mornings or all day Monday and close a little earlier on Saturday. In smaller places shops may close for lunch and on Wednesday or Thursday afternoons. Although the 24/7 culture hasn't yet conquered Belgium, local convenience stores (*magasins de nuit/avondwinkels*) often stay open either all night or until 1:00 or 2:00 a.m., including Sundays. Most family-run stores close for an annual summer vacation of two weeks or more, usually in the first half of August.

Markets

You can find almost anything in a Belgian market—food, antiques, flowers, pets, bric-à-brac—and every town or village has a market at least once a week. The quality of the produce is controlled by health inspectors. Morning markets generally start at dawn and wind down around noon or 1:00 p.m.; afternoon markets begin at 1:00 or 2:00 p.m. and run to 6:00 p.m. or later.

There are over a hundred markets in the Brussels area alone: try the Sunday market around Brussels's Gare du Midi/Zuidstation, the picturesque bird and flower markets on the Grand'Place, the daily flea market at the Place du Jeu de Balle, or the weekend antique and book market at the Place du Grand Sablon. Outside Brussels, on Saturdays you can visit Antwerp's antique and curiosity market, and on Sunday mornings the La Batte antique market at Liège or a lace and old clothes market at Tongeren. For rare and used books, there is Redu in the Ardennes.

Banking

Banking hours are generally Monday to Friday, 9:00 a.m. to 3:30–5:00 p.m. Some banks stay open later on one or two afternoons a week, and some open on a Saturday morning. In smaller towns, banks may close for an hour at lunchtime. If a holiday falls on a weekend, the nearest working day is often taken off. Outside banking hours, foreign exchange kiosks, most big hotels, and travel agents will change money.

Belgium is still a largely cash-based society, preferring money rather than a credit card, especially for small purchases. However, the Proton "electronic purse," a bank card with a computer chip that stores "electronic euros," can be used for small purchases, taxi fares, or telephone calls at Smartcard terminals. Cash dispensers/ATMs are ubiquitous in the major cities and international airports and accept most debit cards. All major credit cards are widely accepted at ATMs, and in restaurants and stores.

EATING AND DRINKING

Dining out is a national pastime, and Belgian cookery is considered to be among the best in the world. Belgium's many restaurants offer not only Wallonian and Flemish cuisine, but just about every kind. Belgium has the world's highest percentage of eateries per capita. It has also collected an impressive number of Michelin stars—eighty were awarded in 2000 alone.

As might be expected, Wallonia and Flanders have different cuisines and regional specialties. Traditional Wallonian cuisine is, like the French, based on rich wine and cream sauces. The Ardennes area is famous for cured ham; *salade wallonie* is a warm salad of lettuce, fried potatoes, and diced bacon. Flemish cuisine, like Dutch, centers on robust stews. Particularly Flemish is *stoemp* (mashed potatoes and other vegetables with sausages or bacon). The national dish, bridging the language divide, is mussels and French fries (*moules et frites*), but mussels are prepared in more than a dozen different ways.

Breakfast in Belgium also reflects the cultural divide. In Flanders, cold meats and cheese accompany a variety of breads, jam, fruit juice, and coffee; Wallonia favors the standard "continental breakfast" of coffee and a croissant or French bread and jam. In Brussels you may get either kind, depending on the price of your accommodation or the origin of the *patron*.

Lunch and dinner are considered of equal importance, with many restaurants offering a *plat du jour/dagschotel* (dish of the day) or a *menu du jour/dagmenu* (menu of the day). Many restaurants have fixed-price menus and a number will have a *menu dégustation/degustatiemenu*, offering small portions of various dishes. Reservations are nearly always necessary, even at noon. Restaurants open for lunch from 11:00 a.m. or noon until 2:00 or 3:00 p.m. Dinner is generally served from 6:30 p.m. to 10:00 or 11:00 p.m. Brasseries, excellent for casual dining, usually open at 11:00 a.m. and stay open until midnight or 1:00 a.m. Hours for cafés and bars are fluid; they open when they like and close when the last customer leaves. Most cafés are open by 10:00 or 11:00 a.m; some do not close until after 3:00 a.m.

When the sun shines, everyone is outside at pavement cafés. There are many types of café in Belgium, but not all serve food. An *estaminet/eetcafe/eetkroeg/* (eating café) will serve beers and a limited selection of meals. A *grand café* is good for a drink or meal at any time. In Flanders, *herbergen* (taverns) are generally larger than ordinary cafés and sometimes serve meals.

In little stands or kiosks on the street, in railway stations, and in shopping centers, you will find two more Belgian national dishes—French fries (*frites/frituur*) and waffles (*gaufres/wafels*). *Frites* (another Belgian invention) are served in a paper cone, usually with mayonnaise.

Drinks

Belgian coffee tends to be strong and espresso-like. If you just ask for *café* or *koffie*, you will get a smallish cup of strong coffee accompanied by a tiny airline-style carton of evaporated milk and a little biscuit, usually a cinnamon-spiced *speculoos*. In Wallonia and Brussels coffee may be served *au lait*, with hot milk. Cappuccino is nearly always topped with artificial whipped cream.

Among alcoholic drinks, beer is king (see box), and is increasingly being exported. The small wine industry in the Hageland region east of Leuven produces good white, rosé, and sparkling wines. There is always a good list of international wines to accompany meals at restaurants.

The Flemings are fond of *jenever* (or *genièvre*), which is similar to gin. Around two hundred and seventy varieties are made in Belgium and most bars will have a good selection. When ordering *jenever* at a bar your best bet is to ask for a *witteke* ("a little white one"), which will come in a tall shot glass cooled in a bed of ice.

Restaurant Etiquette

Service in restaurants is excellent but leisurely, and the more expensive the establishment, the longer your meal will take. For Belgians, eating together is a social occasion. Children accompany their parents even to the best restaurants; they are expected to behave perfectly and generally do.

Dogs are also allowed in most restaurants. Very few restaurants have a nonsmoking area or comply with E.U. ventilation requirements. Interestingly, a recent poll found that 58 percent of Belgians favor a ban on smoking in restaurants and 49 percent would extend this to cafés.

Note that in bars as well as restaurants the waiter will bring your drinks to your table, and you can pay for everything when you leave.

CHEERS!

Belgians have been drinking beer since at least the Middle Ages. St. Arnold is the patron saint of brewers, because, during a fourteenth-century plague epidemic, he persuaded people to drink beer rather than water. Since the beer was boiled and the water was not, a miraculous cure ensued, and Belgians (and many others) have been giving thanks to St. Arnold ever since.

The most common beers are Stella Artois, Jupiler, and Maes, but you won't find them at the specialty beer cafés or pubs. Go to one of these and you'll find a vast menu with several hundred beers. Most cafés will have at least twenty. Never ask for "a beer"—you'll get either a blank stare or a glass of something very basic. You'll need to specify what you want; if in doubt, experiment.

TIPPING

In restaurants a service charge is usually included in the bill. If it is not, a 5 percent or 10 percent tip suffices, but many Belgians do not tip at all unless the service has been exceptionally good. In cafés and snack bars, you can just round up the change.

At both the cinema and the theater, usherettes are there not to help you find your seat but to sell theater programs or hand you a brochure of forthcoming attractions and (except in the largest cinema multiplexes) to collect a tip of €1. Cloakroom attendants and restroom attendants (the latter known locally as Madame Pipi) also both expect to be tipped about €1.

THE ARTS

Every cultural taste is catered to somewhere in Belgium, and most of them in Brussels. Cinemas, homegrown music of all kinds, and resident theater, opera, and dance companies are all well patronized. There are frequent tours by international artists, and a huge number of arts festivals, given the size of the country. The tradition of visual arts, dating back to Van der Weyden, Memlinc, Van Dyck, and Rubens, continues to be vibrant and—particularly in the case of sculpture—publicly visible.

The Belgian state promotes the arts at several levels. The federal government is responsible for national institutions such as the Palais de Beaux Arts/Paleis voor Schone Kunsten and other major museums, the national orchestra, the Monnaie Opera House, and the Royal Library. The regions are responsible for monuments, and the language communities are each responsible for their own cultural policy, administration, and funding.

Sources of information about cultural events, many in English, abound, for instance at the Belgian Tourist Office (www.visitbelgium.com) and the various city tourist offices. The Brussels Tourist Office (TIB) advertises upcoming events in *BBB Agenda* and runs a reservation service for concerts, exhibitions, and theater in Brussels and other major cities. The *Bulletin* contains listings for cultural events in Brussels and further afield.

Major arts festivals include the Brussels KunstenFESTIVALdesArts (May), the annual festivals of Flanders and Wallonia (summer and early fall), the Queen Elisabeth of Belgium International Music Competition, and many international film festivals—and these are just the tip of the iceberg.

Cinema

Belgian cinema tends toward gritty social realism and black humor. The Belgian film industry concentrates on art films, but international mass-market films are shown everywhere and are popular. All cities and most large towns have a modern multiplex center and several also have a small arthouse cinema. A Belgian, Albert Bert, invented the multiplex cinema, and opened the huge twenty-four-screen Kinépolis in Brussels.

Most films are preceded by up to thirty minutes of ads and previews. Particularly on the weekend, it's a good idea to arrive for the whole session (*séance*) to secure a good seat. Besides, Belgian cinema ads can be a good lesson in surrealism.

Films are usually shown in their original language with subtitles in Flanders, and dubbed into French in Wallonia. In listings, VO /OV

 (*version originale/originele versie*) indicates that the film is in its original language, neither dubbed nor subtitled; VO *st-bil*/OV Fr/NL ot. indicates the original version with subtitles in Dutch or French; PF (*parlant français*) or *Vlaamse/Nederlandstalige versie* indicates that French or Dutch have been dubbed in. In French, ENA (*enfants non admis*) indicates that under-sixteens are not admitted; EA (*enfants admis*) means that children of all ages are

admitted. In Dutch, guidance on age is often given in the form "from *x* years" (*vanaf x jaar*).

Annual film festivals include the Brussels International Film Festival and the International Film Festival of Flanders in Ghent. In Brussels, drive-in movie screens are set up in the Parc du Cinquantenaire on weekends in July and August.

Theater

Naturally, major productions are generally staged in French or Dutch, but from time to time there are tours by English-language and other international companies. Despite its name, the newly reopened Théâtre National in Brussels caters only to the French-speaking community; its Dutch-speaking counterpart, the Royal Flemish Theater (Koninklijke Vlaamse Schouwburg, or KVS), is soon to reopen after rebuilding and refurbishment. Other Brussels theaters are the tiny Théâtre de Poche, the Halles de Schaerbeek, and the venerable Théâtre Royal du Parc. Belgium has a strong tradition of marionette theater; the Théâtre Royal de Toone has been run by the Toone family for over a century.

Music, Opera, and Dance

Every kind of live music is available in Belgium, from lunchtime classical concerts to rock music and contemporary jazz. The Belgian National Orchestra performs regularly at the Palais des Beaux-Arts/Paleis voor Schone Kunsten in Brussels.

Brussels's Théâtre Royal de la Monnaie/Koninklijke Muntschouwburg, familiarly known as La Monnaie/De Munt, is the chief opera and ballet venue. Antwerp, Ghent, and Liège have opera houses. The opera season is September to May. Performances generally sell out well in advance to holders of season tickets.

Belgium's contemporary dance companies are among the world's finest. The main ones are Les Ballets C de la B, a "choreographic collective" based in Ghent; Rosas, a Flemish dance company based at La Monnaie; and the avant-garde company Charleroi/Danses–Plan K. Antwerp's resident dance company, the Royal Flanders Ballet, performs at t'Eilandje, a specially built theater. Most companies take a break in July and August.

Fittingly for the country that gave birth to the saxophone (invented by Adolphe Sax in the 1840s), Belgium has a rich jazz culture. Jazz festivals include Jazz Middelheim, a five-day summer festival in Antwerp, the Audi Jazz Festival, and the Brussels Jazz Marathon during the last weekend in May.

The country's biggest rock festival, Rock Werchter, is held at Werchter, near Leuven, in late June or early July. Another annual rock festival,

Pukkelpop, is held in Hasselt in late August.

Watch out for free outdoor music in Brussels, on summer Sundays in the Bois de la Cambre and on the Grand'Place and Place de la Monnaie.

THE ART OF THE COMIC STRIP

The comic strip (*bande dessinée/beeldverhalen*) is called Belgium's "ninth art," some of the most famous Belgians being comic-strip heroes. Forty million comic books are published in Belgium each year. Starting off as an entertainment for children, comics soon became a vehicle for satire and social commentary.

Hergé was the pseudonym of Georges Remi, the creator of *Tintin* (*Kuifje* in Dutch) and father of the Belgian comic strip. By the end of the Second World War a "Belgian school" of comic strip authors was emerging, including Willy Vandersteen, who created *Suske en Wiske* (*Bob et Bobette*), one of Belgium's longest-running comic-book series and the biggest domestic seller. In 1948 Pierre Culliford, known as Peyo, invented *Les Schtroumpf* (the Smurfs).

The golden age of the Belgian comic strip was 1950–70, but the form is still vibrant. Although the main Belgian publishers have been absorbed into large European publishing groups, new Belgian artists still dominate the comics scene.

Museums and Galleries

There are almost three hundred museums in
Belgium, over seventy in the Brussels area alone.
The range of subject matter is vast: from
Renaissance painting to art deco, from chocolate
to the steel industry, from lace to underpants.
Although there is almost more art in Belgium than
you can imagine, and the great Renaissance and
baroque masterpieces are safely housed in famous
galleries, the record of preservation of other
treasures, such as the house of the great art
nouveau architect Victor Horta, is patchy.

SEX *À LA BELGE*

Prostitution is legal in Belgium, but running a
brothel isn't. Yet, in another illustration of the
flexible Belgian approach to regulations, brothels are
big business: in the red-light districts they are in full
view on the street. Proposals are afoot to regulate
prostitution in much the same way as in the
Netherlands, where prostitutes have the same legal
rights as any employee or self-employed person.

Official tolerance of homosexuality in Belgium
is expressed in recent legislation covering same-sex
unions (page 61), but the law does not necessarily
reflect the views of the general public. Gay society
is more or less ignored by heterosexual society,
and the scene is much less prominent than in the

Netherlands. There are gay bars and clubs in major towns and cities, some gay-friendly hotels and a few lesbian café clubs in the larger cities. Antwerp has one of the largest gay nightclubs in Western Europe. The Belgian Gay and Lesbian Pride festival is held on the first Saturday in May.

IN THE COUNTRYSIDE

Cycling and walking are favorite forms of exercise. You will see whole families out for the day, for the flat countryside of Flanders is ideal for cycling, and a network of cycle paths, including some long-distance routes, ensures safety.

Cycling vacations are booming in Flanders, and packages can be organized through Toerisme Vlaanderen. If you prefer to be independent, you can rent bicycles from a railway station and return them to another (but book ahead). A brochure, *Train & Fiets/Train & Vélo*, is available from main stations and gives detailed information. The Ardennes has marked tracks for mountain biking, and bicycles can be rented there too.

Where Flanders favors the cyclist, Wallonia beckons to the walker. Footpaths are excellent and clearly marked. In the Ardennes, there are several long-distance footpaths (*sentiers de grande randonnée*, or just GR), such as the 100-mile (160-km) Transardennaise. The Hautes Fagnes nature reserve is good for short hikes. On some routes there are overnight huts. Hikes in Flanders generally follow cycle paths (walkers give way to cyclists on these). Local tourist offices provide information and sell maps of paths in their area. Specialist hiking maps are produced by the Institut Géographique National (IGN).

Other popular outdoor activities are horse riding, rock climbing, canoeing, kayaking and water skiing, yachting, and angling (a permit is compulsory). Heavy snowfalls in the Ardennes bring out downhill and cross-country skiers. Naturism is popular—surprisingly, perhaps, given the climate

SPORTS

Belgians are passionate about cycle racing, which has given them their greatest sporting hero, Eddy Merckx, five-times winner of the Tour de France. Events take place throughout spring and summer. The biggest traffic-stopper of all (literally—cycling meets have the right of way over other traffic) is *De Gordel* (the Ring), a very Flemish-pride event held on the first Sunday in September around the outer suburbs of Brussels. It is a 100-kilometer (62-mile) cycle ride, but participants also jog or walk. In 2004, over 86,000 people turned out. The Brussels 21-kilometer (13-mile) run, held in the streets of the capital on the last Sunday in May, usually attracts over 20,000 runners.

Tennis has boomed since the emergence of Kim Clijsters and Justine Hénin-Hardenne, ranked as the world's top two women tennis players in 2004. There are public courts, and some private clubs extend midweek privileges to nonmembers.

Belgians are passionate about football, although the national team, the Red Devils (*Diables Rouges/Rode Duivels*), has yet to win a major trophy. The most famous domestic team is RSC Anderlecht, based in Brussels; other top teams are Club Brugge and Standard Liège.

The ancient ball game *balle pelote* is played on the streets of small towns, mostly in Walloon Brabant.

Pigeons have been raced in Belgium since the late eighteenth century, and the sport still has many enthusiasts. The world-governing body for pigeon-racing is in Brussels.

chapter seven

TRAVELING

TRAINS

Belgium was the first country in Europe to have a national railway, and the train is still, by far, the best way of getting around. The railways are run by the Société Nationale des Chemins de Fer Belges (SNCB)/Nationale Maatschappij der Belgische Spoorwegen (NMBS), symbolized by a blue and white "B" in an oval. SNCB offers relatively cheap travel, with several different types of discounted tickets and special deals. There are also combined train/rented cycle or rented car tickets. Tickets can be purchased up to five days in advance but, apart from weekend tickets, there are no open return tickets. Tickets are not on sale on the trains themselves.

Both slow and fast trains go to all big cities; the *stoptrein* can be very slow. Intercity (IC) trains stop at main stations only, interregional (IR) trains also stop at some intermediate stations, local (L) trains stop at all stations, and peak hour (P) commuter trains stop at specific stations only. All the major stations display departure and arrival times prominently. All IC and IR trains run every half hour or hour at the same times past each hour. Smoking has been banned in all trains, but, since Belgians like breaking rules, you may still find your train not entirely smoke-free.

The Euro-Commuter

Large investments in high-speed transportation mean that Brussels is now linked to Paris, Amsterdam, and Cologne by Thalys trains. These fast trains also serve intermediate cities in Belgium, France, the Netherlands, and Germany; with the addition of the Eurostar link with London, Brussels has become the hub for European high-speed rail travel. Every Friday night, thousands of employees stream to London, Paris, Amsterdam, and other cities to go home for the weekend. The number of Euro-commuters is expected to grow; in fact, workers are already commuting from as far afield as Poland to take up job opportunities in Brussels.

BUSES, METRO, AND TRAMS

Belgians tend to use buses only for short journeys, but they are invaluable in rural areas. Buses supplement trains, with services connecting different rail lines or routes branching out from train stations.

Brussels's urban transportation is run by the STIB/MIVB (Société des Transports Intercommunaux Bruxellois/Maatschappij voor het Intercommunaal Vervoer van Brussel) and operates each day from around 6:00 a.m. until midnight, with a reduced service on weekends and public holidays. Route maps of all metro, bus, and tram lines are available from the Brussels Tourist Office or from STIB/MIVB information centers.

The metro is the best way of getting around Brussels. It is modern and efficient, with immaculate stations. The names of the stations are given in both French and Dutch and many are decorated with modern Belgian art. The metro proper consists of three lines linking much of the city. Connecting with this are two complementary tram lines that circulate underground for parts of their route. You can change from a metro to a connecting tram line without leaving the station, simply by changing platforms and boarding a different kind of vehicle. Entrances to metro stations are indicated by a white "M" on a blue background. Color-coded signs inside the station help travelers find their way about.

If you prefer a more scenic and leisurely journey across Brussels or are going to an outer suburb, try the tram network. Several routes continue well out into the suburbs. Yellow STIB/MIVB buses operate across inner Brussels, while orange buses operate in the outlying districts. Tram and bus stops are indicated by red and white signs.

A magnetic card can be bought that is valid for the entire transportation network. Tickets are also available for single trips (*billet simple* or *direct/enkel* or *direct biljet*), five journeys, and ten journeys (*carte de cinq* or *dix trajets/vijf* or *tien ritten kaart*). Each ticket is valid for an hour in any direction, with any number of changes. Tickets must be validated by inserting them into a machine to be stamped each time you enter a station or change from one form of transportation to another (buses and trams have these on board). Inspection is infrequent, but you risk a heavy fine if you don't have a valid ticket.

Antwerp and Ghent have good tram networks. Other cities are served by buses. The Flemish transportation authority, De Lijn, runs a tram service along the coast, called the Kusttram, providing access to resorts not served by trains.

TAXIS

Belgian taxis are among the most expensive in Europe, operating on a fixed-charge basis that includes an initial fee plus a separate charge per kilometer of journey. This charge doubles outside the city limits, and there is a surcharge for journeys after 10:00 p.m. Fares should be on view on the meter beside the driver and there should also be a visible laminated card explaining the fare system. Always check the meter before starting a journey, and if the driver tells you that the meter is broken it's best to take another taxi. Taxes and tips are included in the meter price and requests for extra service charges should be ignored.

Belgian taxi drivers have a reputation for aggressive driving and sometimes argumentative behavior. It is a good idea to carry a street map, as many taxi drivers are foreigners, meaning they often understand only French (Brussels or Wallonia) or only Dutch (Flanders). Unless your destination is well known, they may not know, or may claim not to know, where to go, in order to extract extra charge for a roundabout journey.

BOATS

Belgium has a large network of navigable waterways, over 1,243 miles (2,000 km) in length, of which around 932 miles (1,500 km) are in regular commercial use. Road and rail congestion is prompting a return to the use of canals as freight routes, especially as barges can carry more than trucks. Belgium is part of a long-standing E.U. program to increase the capacity of European inland waterways. The waterways are also used for tourism; boats operate on the River Meuse and a number of other canals and rivers in West Flanders and Hainaut in summer. Small motorboats tour the canals of Bruges and Ghent.

DRIVING

Belgium has many good things, but its drivers are not among them. They are fast, impatient, and sometimes abusive. In fact, driving tests were not introduced until 1967. Until then, you had only to visit the commune, pay a fee, and convince the authorities that you could drive. Today's drivers undergo much more rigorous training, but the resulting indiscipline is uncannily the same.

A Flexible Approach to the Law

Belgium has twice as many road deaths as any of its European neighbors, and the government has implemented new, stiff fines for speeding. Yet, if you idle along an expressway within the speed limit of 75 mph (120 km/h), you are likely to be flashed from behind by drivers doing at least 99 (160). There are speed limits of 56 mph (90 km/h) on other roads, 31 mph (50 km/h) in towns, and 19 mph (30 km/h) on some residential streets.

Speed traps are used, but the police often tell radio stations where they are on a given day. The information is then broadcast, so motorists, forewarned, can cheerfully drive like maniacs elsewhere.

Much the same self-defeating principle seems to apply to alcohol testing. The blood/alcohol limit in Belgium is 0.05 percent—equal to just one glass of wine—but even if you are caught, you can ask the police to give you thirty minutes to mask all traces of alcohol before being tested! Not surprisingly, most Belgians scorn the drunk-driving laws and do not expect to be caught. A high-profile government campaign to reduce drunk driving encourages people at parties to select someone, nicknamed Bob or Bobette (after the comic-strip characters), who will agree to stay sober and be responsible for the driving.

Hazards, Mobile and Otherwise

Belgian cities tend to be congested and full of one-way streets. Always have a streetmap at hand, as road signs are often missing or not well placed. As a result of this, Belgian drivers have perfected the art of the U-turn. Even though traffic police are vigilant about parking, on-street parking is haphazard. Passengers often disembark on to the street rather than the sidewalk, and there is a high chance of collision with cyclists at intersections where vehicles turn right and cross designated cycle lanes. Trams have priority over cars.

Then there is the infamous *priorité à droite/voorrang van rechts* (give way to the right). This gives cars whizzing out from side streets right of way over vehicles on the main road—but not always! If you see signs with an orange-yellow diamond surrounded by white, the main road has priority. Even more confusingly, until recently the *priorité à droite* also applied to roundabouts, vehicles on the roundabout having to give way to incoming traffic. Predictably, this resulted in chaos, so the reverse now applies and roundabout traffic has priority.

In the event of an accident, emergency numbers are 100 for ambulance and 101 for police. Many foreign driver's licenses are honored in Belgium but an international driver's license is recommended, along with motor vehicle insurance with at least third-party coverage. If you bring your own car into Belgium you will need a Green Card confirming that you have adequate coverage, and it is worth having extra insurance for unforeseen legal costs as well as a breakdown policy. The red regulation warning triangle must be carried and displayed in the event of a breakdown. Two national organizations, Touring Club de Belgique and Royal Automobile Club de

Belgique, offer a twenty-four-hour emergency service, but nonmembers will be charged extra.

To rent a car you have to be over twenty-one and have been driving on a current driver's license for at least a year. Rental fees tend to be high.

On weekends or late at night, some gas stations may look shut, but you are still able to use the pumps and pay with a debit card.

Place-names

Never travel around Belgium without a map. Most main cities and towns have both a French and a Flemish name—Antwerpen/Anvers, Brussel/Bruxelles, Gent/Gand, Namur/Namen, and so on. This isn't a real problem until you cross the language divide. In Brussels road signs are bilingual, but outside it they will be in the language of the province you are in, even when directing you to places on the other side of the linguistic fault line. If you are traveling to Mons, for example, you will find that it suddenly disappears and that a new place called Bergen appears on the road signs.

Confusion can also arise with names that refer to both a town and its province (Antwerp, Liège, Namur), and particularly with Luxembourg, which can refer either to a province of Belgium or to the Grand Duchy next door. Be alert—the context will usually make things clear.

CYCLING

Cycling is fine in most cities of Flanders. Ghent has special cycle lanes almost everywhere. The main Walloon cities are less cycle-friendly and in Brussels you take on the taxi drivers, cobblestones, and tram tracks at your peril. The few cycle lanes in Brussels are mostly in the outlying districts. They are usually painted red and marked with white lines. Antwerp motorists seem to be more tolerant, and even though there are not many cycle paths, the city can usually be navigated safely. Away from the cities, the roads are not particularly cycle-friendly, but you are relatively safe, especially on the quiet roads around Bruges, along the coast, and in the Ardennes.

Bicycle theft is common in Belgium as there is apparently no law banning it. Take the necessary precautions and lock up your bike. Antwerp city council has set up *gratis bewaakte fietsenstallingen* —free, supervised parking areas for bikes.

WALKING

Belgians do not like to get out of their cars, so opportunities for pedestrianizing the city centers have not been fully taken up, although there are some attractive pedestrian zones. Brussels still has cobbles, which are picturesque but not easy for walking, and lots of uneven sidewalks.

The Belgian disdain for rules is particularly

evident in the case of parking, which to the pedestrian may seem to happen specifically on pedestrian crossings (marked by a blue triangle). It's best not to assume that these are a safe haven. While traffic lights show the "green man" symbol, traffic is allowed to filter around corners, right into your path as you cross the road. Unlighted crossings are even more of a challenge. Although, by law, drivers must slow down or stop to let pedestrians cross, you are more likely to get an indignant glare than a smile from motorists.

Finally, and regretfully, no account of getting around Brussels would be complete without a word of warning about the city's most insidious hazard—dog mess, at its worst in middle-class suburban parks. In 2003 Brussels introduced a heavy fine for dog fouling, but there is little evidence yet of this having been enforced.

WHERE TO STAY

Hotels in Belgium cover the usual range from expensive and luxurious to cheap and simple, some offering reduced rates for long stays. The Belgian Tourist Reservations Service (BTR) produces a list of approved hotels and relevant prices (not in English). You can book hotel rooms nationwide through the Belgian Tourist Office. Information can also be found on many Web sites, including www.hotelconnect.com/belgium. Belgium uses the Benelux Standard to classify its hotels or guesthouses, which are licensed by the appropriate government agency. Grades range from one to five stars. The system is based on facilities rather than location and cost.

B & Bs (*gastenkamers/chambres d'hôtes*) have become very popular in recent years, although many tend to be situated away from city centers or on the second floor of town houses with no elevators. Residential apartment hotels, often called flat-hotels or *résidences*, offer weekly or monthly rates, and are a good short-term housing option. In the countryside, guesthouses or apartments are known as *landelijke verblijven/gîtes ruraux*, and are often attached to farms; or you can stay *en famille* in a farmhouse itself—a good way to meet local people.

Belgium has quite a lot of HI (Hostelling International) registered youth hostels (*auberges de jeunesse/jeugdherbergen*). These are run by two separate organizations, one for Flanders and one for Wallonia. Both operate also in Brussels. In the remoter rural areas of Wallonia you may stumble across *gîtes d'étapes*. These are generally aimed at groups and have dormitory-style accommodation with kitchen facilities.

Camping is extremely popular in Belgium and there are hundreds of campsites to choose from. A similar grading system to hotels is used, graded one-star to five-star, based on facilities.

SAFETY AND SECURITY

Belgium is generally a safe country to travel in. The crime rate is low, and the main risk for a traveler is probably that of a road accident, though it is wise to beware of pickpockets in the bleak passages of Brussels's main stations and the back-streets of the tourist-thronged area around the Grand'Place. You may also be importuned by street performers, and there is some begging on the metro and in the streets.

Identity Documents

Every Belgian has an identity card from the age of twelve. Foreign residents over fifteen carry them too; they are issued together with residence permits. The ID card is accepted as a way of being able to prove who you are. In a road accident, for instance, Belgians show each other their ID cards. As a tourist, you are required to carry your passport or other identification with you at all times. The federal government is eager to introduce electronic ID cards throughout Belgium. However, many communes are resisting this on grounds of expense.

If you intend to stay in Belgium for longer than three months, you will need a residence permit, and if you intend to work you will need a work permit. Different conditions apply to E.U. and non-E.U. citizens. The Belgian embassy in your home country will advise you about these. According to a recent E.U. directive, E.U. citizens no longer need to apply for residence in other E.U. member states, but some documentation may continue to be necessary.

The Police

Driving is the activity most likely to bring you into contact with the Belgian police. The police force was restructured in 2000–01 following the outcry against police incompetence and corruption in 1996. The local police regulate local traffic and enforce parking regulations, while the federal police are responsible for patrolling highways, which they often do in unmarked cars. If you are unlucky enough to be robbed or burgled, you will need to make a declaration at the nearest police station, where you will receive the documentation necessary for an insurance claim.

chapter eight

BUSINESS BRIEFING

Belgium's economy today is very diverse, with large and small businesses operating in many sectors. At the beginning of 2005 confidence in the country's economy was high. Belgium's strategic position in Europe and its long history of trading make its business community very open to opportunities and internationalist in outlook; this may have resulted in the past in the submersion of Belgian interests in multinational corporations based outside the country. Many of the enterprises started up in the early twentieth century now belong only partly, if at all, to Belgian interests.

FAMILY FIRMS AND MULTINATIONALS

There are thriving businesses in both the domestic and multinational sectors. Around 70 percent of enterprises in Belgium with over 1,000 employees are owned by multinational corporations. These include many of the world's household names.

Family businesses are the backbone of the domestic sector, making up at least 70 percent of small and medium-sized enterprises. Family firms run a kaleidoscope of enterprises ranging from restaurants and chocolate factories to furniture and interior design stores, and even a few of Belgium's hundred remaining breweries. The interests of the small family firm sector are strongly promoted by the oddly named Ministry of the Middle Classes.

GOVERNMENT AND BUSINESS

Although foreign investment is important and the government is eager to encourage it, the many levels of administration generate a highly complex and reduplicative bureaucracy that can be off-putting to investors. In 2003–04, the government carried out a consultation exercise called "Kafka," designed to find ways of cutting red tape. Its main conclusions, however, were that the levels of government needed to coordinate better, and that "e-government" should be developed. In practice, the bureaucracy can be so stifling, and the spirit of compromise can slow down decision making to such an extent, that businesses often simply sidestep the processes. This rather Latin approach to bureaucracy, however, doesn't mean that Belgians are not serious and hardheaded about conducting business. And *le compromis belge* does mean that they respond positively and creatively to negotiation and dialogue.

One area where the government is particularly interested in regulation is corporate social responsibility. This springs from its concern with employment, harmonious labor relations, and strong social cohesion. The federal government has passed a law, applying to both domestic and multinational companies, to promote socially responsible production in line with International Labour Organization standards. This can cause problems, however. In 2004 the federal government was split over whether to allow the courier DHL to expand its operations at Brussels airport, with Flemish and Liberal Party politicians favoring the move because it would bring thousands of jobs, and Walloons and Socialists opposing it on the grounds of increased noise pollution from night flights. Talks went on for weeks—consensus-building, or indecisiveness?

THE BELGIAN WORKFORCE

Belgian workers are among the world's most productive. At the same time, the working week is fairly short, there are numerous public holidays, and Belgians do not allow their work and home lives to overlap much; taking work home on the weekend, for instance, is a sign of desperation.

It appears, too, that Belgians are extremely loyal to their jobs, if they are happy in them, and job turnover is not high, even if the economy is favorable. While this might signal a lack of dynamism in the work culture, it also means greater institutional continuity than in situations of constant staff turnover.

The public sector is large, because of the language-based duplications. At higher levels in particular, political affiliations have historically been influential in appointments, and politically awarded sinecures in ministries were common. There has been legislation to regulate this kind of activity, but it has not totally disappeared.

As we have seen, labor relations in Belgium are based on dialogue. About 60 percent of workers are unionized. Social dialogue between trade unions, employers, and government has been called "the incarnation of Belgian compromise," and a high level of harmonization is seen as essential to head off or neutralize disagreement.

WOMEN IN BUSINESS

Despite the favorable official climate for women's employment, which must take some of the credit for the high percentage (just over 50 percent) of women in professional and technical jobs, women still occupy only 3 percent of corporate boardroom seats in Belgium. However, foreign businesswomen are usually welcomed in Belgium, especially in the more cosmopolitan cities. They may find they are treated with a fair amount of old-fashioned gallantry, but it is also acceptable for a foreign woman to invite Belgian colleagues of either sex to dinner, and to pay the bill.

Sexual harassment in the workplace is prohibited by law.

MANAGEMENT STYLES

The leadership styles of Belgian senior managers combine, in varying proportions, the authoritative (but not authoritarian) and the consultative or democratic. But, as usual, differences between Flemish and Walloon practice can be detected, and because of these differences, it is difficult to generalize. Walloon managers tend to prefer formal

organization and hierarchical company structures and systems, with clear top-down leadership and sensitivity to titles and rank. People are very aware of their place in the corporate pecking order. In Flanders, by contrast, company structures, like the landscape, are generally much flatter, although not completely horizontal. Participatory management, consensus building, and delegation of responsibility are important values in the workplace, and the management style is more open to individual initiative.

DOING BUSINESS: A MINI-GUIDE

These suggestions apply chiefly to the specific business cultures of Belgium, since the corporate culture of the multinationals is international.

The basic rule is that you should always keep in mind Belgium's dual (or triple) culture and approach each culture appropriately. Try to find out about the people you will be talking to or working with and you will be less likely to make a gaffe. Also, remember that Belgium is small. Everyone in a particular business field probably knows everyone else (at least within the language community), so sensitivity is crucial.

Making Contacts and Appointments

Never show up without warning. Write or call at least a week in advance to introduce yourself and your company and to make an appointment. Reconfirm your appointment by telephone, fax, or e-mail a couple of days before the meeting.

Watch the Time!

In Dutch the half hour is counted *before* the hour, not after it: *half negen* means 8:30, not 9:30. You should therefore never say "half nine" if you mean "half past nine." Your Flemish counterpart will probably arrive for the meeting at 8:30, and have left in a huff or be involved in other work by the time you get there at 9:30.

Be punctual. Without exception. Belgians, especially Walloons, have many "Latin" characteristics, but being late is not one of them. Don't arrive too early, either; rather than commendably eager, you will look as though you're trying to upstage the staff.

Top brass tend to come in to the office later than their staff. If you are seeing a senior person, mid-morning or mid-afternoon are the most likely times for meetings. Do not expect to be invited to a power breakfast!

Language

Understanding the linguistic divide is as fundamental in business relations as anywhere else in Belgium. Above all, don't speak or present literature in the wrong language! Don't address Flemings in French (they will be insulted), or Walloons in Dutch (they may not understand you), or German Belgians in either. Fortunately, there is English, increasingly a lingua franca in business—but don't assume that everyone will automatically be happy with this. Always ask first if the meeting can be conducted in English.

Dress Code

On the whole, Belgians dress conservatively. It is important to dress fairly formally for a business meeting, particularly your first with a client. That means suits and ties for men and suits or tailored jackets, with either trousers or skirts, for women. You can expect to be judged at least partly by your taste in clothes. Ostentation will not send the right message; quiet elegance and good grooming will.

Business Cards

Present your card when meeting people for business purposes. Business cards in English are acceptable, but cards printed in English on one side and French or Dutch on the other make a better impression. If you are a married woman, use both your maiden and your married names—Belgian women don't change their surnames when they marry.

WHICH IS WHICH?

Many Flemish people and companies have apparently French names, and vice versa. But you can tell the difference by the letters after a company's name. Flemish firms are either NV (*Naamloze Vennootschap*) or BVBA (*Besloten Vennootschap met Beperkte Aansprakelijkheid*); Walloon companies are SA (*Société anonyme*) or SPRL (*Société privée à responsabilité limitée*).

Meetings

Remember to shake hands with everyone present
at a meeting, at the beginning and when you leave.
Repeat your name when being introduced. (It is
also ill-mannered, when answering the telephone,
just to say, "Hello," and not give your name.)

If you are visiting an office, don't just walk in.
This may be impossible in any case, as senior
managers in particular value their privacy and
open-plan offices are not very common.

If you are calling a meeting, it is efficient to
draw up an agenda and give a copy
to everyone attending. Your efforts
to keep the meeting focused and on
time will also be appreciated.

Marshal your facts and figures
and be prepared to present them
clearly. Belgians appreciate good
empirical evidence to back up the
case being made. They will also be interested in
concrete ideas and practical solutions to any
problems that arise. Choose common sense over
spin every time.

Never interrupt a meeting to receive—and
especially not to make—a call on your cell phone.

Negotiation and Decision Making

Belgians like to get to know whom they will be
doing business with, so your first meeting with a

new contact may be low-key and devoted to making social contact. For the same reason you should not be surprised if a meeting or negotiation seems to take a long time to get beyond the initial small talk. It is all part of the building of trust that Belgian businesspeople feel should underpin business relationships.

Your interlocutors are likely to seek compromise and consensus rather than be confrontational. Some Belgians say this is a key difference between them and the Dutch. A calm negotiating style, patience, and readiness to concede points will always get you further in Belgium than aggression or an immovable bottom line. This can mean, however, that decision making is slow, as every point of view is considered and consensus is built.

Decisions are made differently in Flemish and Walloon contexts: in Wallonia, even after long discussion, the final decision is usually made by the most senior person involved, while in less hierarchical Flanders decisions are more likely to be reached by consensus.

The Business Lunch

Lunch is the meal for doing business in Belgium; dinner is usually a purely social occasion. If you have been invited to a Belgian home for dinner, remember that Belgians like to close the door on work at the end of the day. By the same token, don't call a Belgian business associate at home on business matters if you can possibly avoid it.

Always treat a business lunch seriously; you may learn things there that you would not learn at a meeting or in an office. At the same time, the atmosphere of ease and confidentiality should not lull you into speaking indiscreetly or behaving carelessly. A successful lunch may clinch a deal.

By British or U.S. standards, a lunch appointment can begin very early and take up quite a lot of the afternoon. In fact any morning appointment from 11:30 a.m. onward should be regarded as a lunch appointment, and you should be prepared to organize your day around it.

If you are hosting a lunch, it is a good idea to reserve a table; if you can't, be aware that restaurants fill up quickly for lunch and make sure you get to your chosen restaurant by about 12:30.

Follow-up

Obviously, your business relationships will not end the moment you sign the deal or leave the country. You will have assured your Belgian clients or counterparts that you will follow up on all decisions made, meet the necessary deadlines, and stay in touch; so it is a good strategy, and will show that you are serious, to send a letter as soon as you get home reiterating these assurances and thanking those you have met for their time and their contributions. It is also acceptable to send Christmas or New Year greeting cards to business colleagues as a way of staying in touch.

MEETING THE E.U. INSTITUTIONS

We have mentioned the prevalence of political and business lobbying in Brussels, mostly directed at the E.U. institutions. In fact, lobbying is now a business in itself. The expansion of the E.U. is expected to lead to greater regulation of lobbyists.

If you are meeting representatives of the E.U. institutions, you will probably find the experience differs from meetings with businesspeople. It is vital to contact in advance the person you want to meet, and to confirm the appointment by phone or e-mail. Whichever institution you visit, you will be asked by security to leave your passport at the front desk while you are in the building.

As in the commercial context, prompt and meaningful follow-up is important. Keep your E.U. contacts informed of any process set in motion by your visit.

chapter nine

COMMUNICATING

WHICH LANGUAGE?

At the risk of repetition, let us remind visitors to
be immensely careful never to address any Belgian
in the wrong language. This can be tricky, because
people's names are not always identifiably either
Flemish or Walloon. If in doubt, ask if you may
speak English. English is fast acquiring the status
of a lingua franca in Belgium,
particularly in Brussels and
Flanders. International business
is carried out in it, the E.U. uses
it as much as French as a default
language, schoolchildren in all
parts of the country would rather
learn English than the language of the
other half of their own country.

You will possibly be told "helpfully" that
different institutions in bilingual Brussels prefer
different languages—speak Dutch or English at
the airport, French at the station, for instance—
but the only hard-and-fast rule seems to be that
whatever language you use to speak to the guard

on a train out of Brussels—French, Dutch, or English—he will answer you in another.

WRITTEN COMMUNICATION

In Belgium, in both Dutch and French, written communication tends to be more formal than verbal. If you are writing in English, you won't be able to use formal phrases of the same kind as in French or Dutch, so be as polite as possible. Also, don't assume that your addressee either has perfect idiomatic English or is a mere beginner. Write clearly, concisely, and simply, without being condescending. Remember that nuance is harder to judge in writing than face-to-face, and avoid irony and ambiguities unless you are writing to someone you know, and who knows English well.

E-mail falls somewhere between written and spoken conversation. There is a surprising amount of debate about how formal e-mails should be in a work setting, especially where, as in Belgium, office relations are fairly hierarchical and bosses do not see themselves as the equals of their staff. Sensitivity to tone in your e-mails—and, of course, using the correct language—is key.

Forms of Address

The standard abbreviated titles used in addressing letters in French and Dutch are, respectively,

M./Meneer (Mr.), *Mme/Mevr.* (Mrs.), *Mlle/Mej.*
(Miss), and *Mw.* (Ms.). There is no French
equivalent of "Ms."; just use *Mme.*

Both French and Dutch use different words for
the singular and the plural "you," used formally
and informally. In Dutch the formal "you" is *u*,
both singular and plural, and is safest to use (as
well as being easiest to remember) in a formal
setting or with someone you don't know very well:
you will hear it all the time in phrases such as *dank
u* (thank you) and *alstublieft* (please—literally, "If
you please"). The informal forms are *je* (singular)
and *jullie* (plural), and were used until not too long
ago only when speaking to close family and friends,
or children, but are now more widely used among
friends and even acquaintances. If you've been
invited to call someone by his or her first name,
you can use the *je* form.

In French the usage is much the same: use *vous*
(plural, and formal singular) until you are invited
to use the informal singular *tu*. The verbs
describing these practices are *tutoyer* (to use *tu*)
and *vousvoyer* (to use *vous*).

Although it is increasingly common for colleagues
to use first names and familiar pronouns at work, it
is far less often done when there is a significant
difference in age or position and when talking to
"outsiders" such as clients or suppliers. As a rule, it is
best to wait until invited to move to a more intimate

level of address with any Belgian acquaintance. You are more likely to be invited to *tutoyer* and use first names by a Fleming than a Walloon. French speakers from Brussels are the least likely to initiate familiarities, perhaps because so many encounters in Brussels are professional and transitory.

FACE-TO-FACE
Greetings

You will find yourself shaking hands a lot in your meetings with Belgians, not only when you are being introduced to someone but when greeting or saying good-bye as well. At a business meeting, you should shake hands with everyone there on arriving and leaving. Kissing the cheeks, or air kissing, is also frequent among people who know each other well. The number of kisses given each time is usually three but can vary—take your cue from your Belgian acquaintance. Two men will usually just shake hands, but don't slap anyone heartily on the back—not good form.

It is polite to greet staff in small shops (from the local bakery to the upmarket boutiques in the Avenue Louise), at the supermarket checkout, at the post office counter, in restaurants, and so on. You should say "good morning/afternoon/ evening" (*bonjour, bonsoir*/*goede morgen, goede middag, goeden avond*) when you enter and "good-bye" (*au revoir* or *bonjour* again/*goedendag* or just *dag*) when you leave, but always add *Monsieur, Madame, Mademoiselle*, or their Dutch equivalents *Meneer, Mevrouw*, or *Mejuffrouw* after the word of greeting. The assistants will probably greet you first, which makes it easier to return their greeting.

Note that the French *Mademoiselle* is much less commonly used now that it has been accepted that defining a woman's marital status is irrelevant, especially in professional contexts, but is reserved for girls and very young women not in positions of authority, such as students and junior staff.

The Flemish are much more punctilious about saying please and thank you than the Dutch—you will constantly hear *alstublieft*, meaning not only "please" but, effectively, "you're welcome," said politely to someone who has just thanked you.

Body Language

Belgians are easy to talk to, friendly, and funny, but they are not physically demonstrative on the whole. Apart from greetings, you should always give personal space to the person you are talking to and restrain yourself from touching people as you talk to them. Antwerp is the place where you are most likely to see large Italianate gestures and physical exuberance; other Flemings think the Antwerpers brash and loud, and a bit louche.

Certain gestures or habits are considered vulgar or rude: snapping your fingers, yawning, sneezing or blowing your nose in public, pointing with your forefinger, keeping your hands in your pockets while conversing, putting your hands in your lap while at table, chewing gum.

MEDIA

You won't be surprised to learn that there are two networks, one French-speaking and one Dutch-speaking, for every aspect of the Belgian media. TV personalities, popular musicians, and journalists tend to be known in their own region (and in Holland and France respectively) but not across the language fault line.

Newspapers and Magazines

The readership and circulation of newspapers has been declining, particularly since the Internet and digital television became universally available. Among those who do read newspapers, most tend to be more interested in local news and gossip than in international news and analysis. The most widely read paper is *La Dernière Heure des Sports*, a populist tabloid-style paper.

The main quality papers are, in Flanders, *De Standaard* (very Flemish) and *De*

Morgen (left-wing with a good reputation for investigative journalism), and in Wallonia *Le Soir* (center-right, fairly neutral) and *La Libre Belgique* (also center-right, serious, very Catholic). There are a couple of business-oriented newspapers (*L'Echo de la Bourse* and *De Financieel-Ekonomische Tijd*), and English-language papers are widely read, especially in Brussels, where a wide range is on most newsstands. *European Voice*, an English-language paper with an E.U. focus, is published in Brussels.

Many weekly magazines of both general and special interest are published in both languages. They include *Le Soir Illustré*, *Ciné Télé Revue* (containing cinema and TV features and program listings for the whole country), and *Dag Allemaal* (a Flemish version of *Hello!* magazine focusing on Flemish celebrities). *Humo* gives an irreverent, highly intelligent analysis of news and culture. The English-language weekly *The Bulletin* is a key source for expatriates on Belgian current affairs, cultural news, listings, and relevant advertising.

Broadcast Media

The public TV and radio networks are RTBF (Radio télévision belge de langue française) in French and VRT (Vlaamse Radio- en Televisieomroep) in Dutch. RTBF television channels are RTBF 1 (known as "*la une*")

 and 2 ("*la deux*"); VRT has TV1, Ketnet (youth-centered), and Canvas (cultural news and features). Belgians have had access to cable TV since the 1960s, and a large majority of homes receive both domestic and foreign channels.

VRT Radio has five radio stations for the Flemish audience and a worldwide service, Radio Vlaanderen Internationaal, broadcasting in Dutch, French, English, and German. RTBF has a similar network. Both broadcast news, sports, classical and popular music, and other features. There are also plenty of commercial radio stations.

The Internet

Over 40 percent of the population are regular Internet users. You can find numerous Web sites devoted to information for foreigners in Belgium; two of the most interesting available in early 2005 are Expatica.com and EurActiv.com.

MAIL

Post offices are usually open from 9:00 a.m. to 5:00 p.m. on weekdays and 9:00 a.m. to noon on Saturdays. In smaller towns, post offices, like banks, close for lunch. Within Belgium mail can be delivered promptly overnight, but the postal service to other countries is slow. Although there are two rates for sending mail—*prioritaire* (priority) and *non-prioritaire* (non-priority)—most Belgians would never contemplate the non-priority option: too many delays.

In Flanders, street numbers follow the street name in addresses (e.g., Tiensestraat 183). In Wallonia and Brussels addresses are in French; the number can follow or precede the street name. A four-digit post code, sometimes preceded by "B-", precedes the city or town name in either language (e.g., 3000-Leuven or B-3000 Leuven). "Van" in names is capitalized in Belgium, not in the Netherlands. It's easiest to buy stamps at the post office (they can be bought at vending machines) because the pricing system is complicated. Use Belgian envelopes, as you may have to pay more if your envelope doesn't pass the standard size test.

The post office also offers a full banking service, including bill payment and traveler's check encashment, and numerous other services.

TELEPHONE

Telephone services were privatized in 2001, but the former national company Belgacom is still the main provider and is relatively efficient. Public phones are few and far between and mostly take phone cards or credit cards, rarely coins. If you are not resident in Belgium, your simplest option, apart from a mobile phone, is to buy a Belgacom XL-Call telephone card from a railway station, newsdealer, post office, or supermarket. Phones marked with European flags can be used for direct-dialed calls to other countries.

Belgium is part of the GSM cell phone network, which operates in most of Western Europe. Calls are very expensive. If you are staying in a hotel, check carefully whether it would not be cheaper to use the hotel phone and pay its rates than to make international calls on your mobile.

Belgium's Yellow Pages directory is called *Pages Jaunes/Gouden Gids*, and the directory inquiries number is 1405 (operates in English).

ANSWERING THE TELEPHONE

When answering the telephone it is considered impolite not to give your name. In Dutch you say "*Met* Ann Smith" ("With Ann Smith," or "Ann Smith here") or, if you prefer first-name terms, "*Met* Ann." In fact, you can omit "Hello" altogether. In French, the name is usually said first—"Ann Smith, *bonjour.*"

CONCLUSION

Throughout this book we have necessarily dealt in generalizations, in order to give a broad picture and a guide that is generally applicable. You will probably find exceptions to every "rule" mentioned here—indeed, Belgium would be far less fascinating if you didn't.

The globalization of communication through mass media, the Internet, and multinational business means that culture and customs are changing fast in Belgium, as elsewhere, and in many ways local characteristics are at risk of flattening out into a kind of international norm. Nevertheless, much of what seems most Belgian about the Belgians—their astonishing architecture, their weird folkloric festivals, their historical tenacity, their absurdist wit, their political model of bridging difference by compromise, their love of the good life—continues to resist globalization and to enrich the cultural fabric of Europe.

Belgium is a country that never ceases to surprise. It has absorbed something of each of the cultures that have invaded it during its history and—despite the Francophone and Flemish linguistic and cultural divide—combines the pragmatic and the surreal, individual reserve and artistic flamboyance, in a way that is unmistakably Belgian. Boring? We think not.

Further Reading

This list does not include readily available English-language tourist guides. The *Everyman Guide to Brussels and Southern Belgium* (London: David Campbell, 1996) has an excellent bibliography of works in English.

Ascherson, Neal. *The King Incorporated: Leopold the Second and the Congo.* London: Granta Books, 1999.

Blom, J.C.H., Emiel Lamberts, and James C. Kennedy. *History of the Low Countries.* New York/Oxford: Berghahn Books, 1999.

Brontë, Charlotte. *Villette* (ed. Tony Tanner). London: Penguin, 1985. (Brontë's last novel, set in Belgium in a fictional town called Villette.)

Blyth, Derek. *Brussels for Pleasure.* London: Pallas Athene, 2003.

——. *Flemish Cities Explored.* 4th ed. London: Pallas Athene, 1999.

Claus, Hugo. *The Sorrow of Belgium.* Woodstock, NY: Overlook Press, 2002. First published in Dutch as *Het verdriet van België* (Amsterdam: De Bezige Bij, 1983). (Widely considered to be Belgium's greatest novel. Set against the background of the Second World War and collaboration with the Germans.)

De Vries, Andre, and Greg Adams. *Live and Work in Belgium, the Netherlands and Luxembourg.* Oxford: Vacation Work Publications, 1998.

Elliott, Mark. *Culture Shock! Belgium: A Guide to Customs and Etiquette.* Portland, Oregon: Graphic Arts Center Publishing Company, 2002/ London: Kuperard, 2002.

Friedlander, Max. *From Van Eyck to Bruegel.* London: Phaidon Press, 1998. (First published 1956. A classic account of the art of the Flemish Renaissance.)

Kapstein, Nancy (ed.). *Hints for Living in Belgium.* Brussels: American Women's Club of Brussels (first published 1951).

Nicholas, David. *Medieval Flanders.* London/New York: Longman, 1993.

Pearson, Harry. *A Tall Man in a Low Land: Some Time among the Belgians.* London: Abacus, 1999.

The Low Countries: Art and Society in Flanders and the Netherlands. Yearbook published by the Flemish–Netherlands Foundation Stichting Ons Erfdeel. (The Foundation also publishes the bilingual yearbook *De Franse Nederlanden – Les Pays-Bas Français* and a cultural quarterly, *Septentrion*. See www.onserfdeel.be/en/default.asp.)

Van Istendael, Geert. *Het Belgisch Labyrinth of De Schoonheid der Wanstaltigheid* (*The Belgian Labyrinth, or the Beauty of Deformity*). Amsterdam: De Arbeiderspers, 1989. In Dutch. French translation, *Le labyrinthe belge*, by Monique Nagielkopf and Vincent Marnix, with preface by Jacques De Decker (Pantin: Le Castor Astral, 2004; Escales du Nord series).

Witte, Els, Jan Craeybeckx, and Alain Meynen. *Political History of Belgium from 1830 Onwards* (trans. Raf Casert). Amsterdam: VU University Press, 2001.

Index

Acknowledgments

In writing this book I have relied on information and support from many people, but it really could not have been written without the contributions of An Smout, Manuel Muñoz, Bénédicte Allaert, and in particular my husband, Graham Denyer. My heartfelt thanks to you all.